# Mastering HR Challenges

*A Comprehensive Guide for Human Resource Professionals*

**Koren A. Norton, MSW,CEAP**

**Elijah M. James, Ph. D.**

Canadian Cataloguing in Publication Data
Koren A. Norton & Elijah M. James
Mastering HR Challenges: A Comprehensive Guide for Human Resource Professionals

ISBN 978-1-0690086-6-4

EJ Publishing
603 White Plains Run
Hammonds Plain
Nova Scotia, Canada    B4B 1W7

This book is dedicated to the HR professionals who drive change, support growth, and bring compassion to every corner of the workplace. Your work is the backbone of successful organizations, and your dedication to people makes all the difference. This book is for you—may it serve as a valuable tool and an acknowledgment of the incredible impact you make every day.

# Table of Contents

# Preface

For over five decades, we have had the privilege of working as HR consultants, guiding organizations through the complexities of managing people. We have seen firsthand the pivotal role Human Resources plays in shaping an organization's culture, success, and sustainability. HR professionals are not merely administrative support; they are strategic partners responsible for nurturing talent, resolving conflicts, and ensuring the overall well-being of employees. Yet, the challenges HR managers face are numerous and often overwhelming—from recruiting and retaining top talent to addressing absenteeism, employee engagement, compliance, and workplace relationships.

This book, *Mastering HR Challenges: A Comprehensive Guide for Human Resource Professionals*, was born out of our experiences dealing with these challenges and our desire to equip HR officers with practical tools and insights to overcome them. Throughout our careers, we have witnessed the evolving landscape of HR—from the traditional personnel department to the strategic powerhouse it is today. We understand that no two challenges are alike, but we also know that there are

1

proven principles and strategies that can help HR professionals handle even the toughest situations.

Each chapter in this book addresses a critical HR issue, providing a deep dive into its causes, effects, and most importantly, actionable solutions. Whether it's creating a positive workplace culture, managing conflict, implementing diversity and inclusion programs, or preparing for the future of work, this guide is designed to be a resource that HR professionals can turn to in moments of need.

The glossary of terms at the end of the book serves as a valuable reference tool for readers to quickly understand industry-specific language and concepts. In the field of Human Resources, terms can be complex or used differently across organizations, so a glossary provides clear definitions to ensure readers, whether seasoned HR professionals or newcomers, have a consistent understanding of essential topics. By offering easy access to definitions, the glossary supports readers in fully comprehending the book's content, enhancing their ability to apply insights and strategies effectively in real-world HR situations.

*Mastering HR Challenges* stands out by focusing directly on real-world issues and providing actionable solutions tailored to today's dynamic workplace environment. Unlike many traditional HR texts, which often emphasize theoretical frameworks, this book prioritizes practical strategies for handling specific challenges like absenteeism, talent retention, and employee engagement. With insights from experienced

HR professionals and case studies from diverse industries, *Mastering HR Challenges* equips readers with the tools needed to resolve the most pressing workforce issues effectively.

We hope this book will not only provide answers but also inspire HR professionals to see themselves as catalysts for positive change within their organizations. HR is about more than managing people—it's about unlocking the potential in every individual and creating an environment where both employees and organizations can thrive.

May this book serve as a trusted companion as you continue your journey to mastering the ever-changing world of Human Resources.

# **Acknowledgements**

Writing *Mastering HR Challenges* has been an experience of shared insights, guidance, and the invaluable support of many dedicated individuals. This book would not have been possible without the contributions of the HR professionals who so generously shared their personal experiences and challenges with us. Your openness and willingness to discuss both triumphs and obstacles have added depth, authenticity, and richness to this work, transforming it into a resource that speaks to the heart of what it means to be an HR professional today.

We are profoundly grateful to our colleagues and other experts in the HR field who offered their thoughtful feedback and constructive comments. Your insights and perspectives have been instrumental in shaping this book, ensuring it is both comprehensive and practical for those dealing with complex HR landscapes.

We owe a debt of gratitude to Ms. Heidi Skerrett for her invaluable contribution to *Mastering HR Challenges*. Her keen insights and thoughtful suggestions on a section of our work added depth and clarity, enhancing its overall impact. Her expertise and attention to detail have truly enriched this book, and we are deeply appreciative of her time and commitment. Thank you, Heidi, for your support and guidance.

To everyone who has contributed in any way—whether through advice, encouragement, or behind-the-scenes support—we extend my heartfelt thanks. Your dedication to the HR profession and commitment to fostering positive change are an inspiration. This book is a testament to the collective wisdom and unwavering resilience of our community, and we are honored to have been part of this journey with you.

Thank you all for helping bring *Mastering HR Challenges* to life.

*Koren A. Norton*
*Elijah M. James*

# INTRODUCTION

How do you keep your workforce engaged, productive, and resilient in a world where workplace expectations change so rapidly?

How do you, as an HR professional, manage your role while answering to management, placating unions, and trying to please staff?

Human resource professionals face so many challenges that stretch across recruitment, retention, diversity, remote work, and compliance that your role demands a unique combination of skills, empathy, strategy, and adaptability.

We know you wear many hats— you are assessors, recruiters, problem-solvers, legal experts, counselors, mediators, strategists, and employee advocates; and these roles have become increasingly complex, with each new challenge demanding a refined skill set and a deep understanding of best practices.

*Mastering HR Challenges: A Comprehensive Guide for Human Resource Professionals* was written because having worked with HR professionals for many years, we saw the challenges you faced and we wanted to provide tools that are made up of proven strategies to help you thrive no matter the industry, whether you lead a team of 12 or 1200.

This book is organized into twenty detailed chapters, each focused on a critical area of human resources. From Understanding and Reducing Absenteeism in Chapter 1 to The Future of Human Resources in Chapter 20, this guide spans almost the entire HR spectrum. We hope that in each chapter, you find clear, practical guidance on issues that you encounter daily, along with long-term strategies to help your organization remain competitive and resilient in the face of change.

As workplaces continue to evolve with advancements in technology, shifting workforce demographics, and increasing attention to employee well-being, HR professionals must adapt, embracing both new skills and mindsets. It won't always be easy, but understand that people are dynamic, and as an HR professional, you must be a leader. You will have to model what you preach and you will have to make some difficult decisions, but at the end of the day, ensure that your actions and behavior are in alignment with your core values and the mission of the organization you represent. Our aim is that this book is a valuable companion, helping you become a forward-thinking leader capable of shaping the future of work.

# CHAPTER 1
# UNDERSTANDING AND REDUCING ABSENTEEISM

*Healthier employees mean happier employees. There's less absenteeism, improved productivity and lowered health care premium costs.*—**Jim Link**

Julia, a project manager, noticed that her team was struggling because of frequent absences from her teammate, Sam. At first, his sporadic days off seemed manageable, but soon deadlines slipped, client frustrations grew, and the team's morale took a hit as they picked up his slack.

When Julia approached Sam, he revealed he'd been juggling personal issues and burnout. With HR's help, Sam adjusted his schedule, taking regular mental health days without seriously affecting the team. The simple act of support restored balance, showing Julia that absenteeism often signals a need for empathy and resources rather than just discipline.

Absenteeism is a critical challenge for organizations of all sizes and industries. Defined as the frequent or habitual absence of employees from their work, absenteeism can impact everything from team dynamics and morale to organizational productivity and profitability. While occasional absences are to be expected, consistent and unplanned absenteeism can signify deeper issues within the workplace or individual employee struggles that need to be addressed.

This chapter examines the multifaceted nature of absenteeism, examining the reasons behind it and the tangible effects it has on productivity. We will explore strategies to encourage attendance, including identifying root causes, developing supportive policies, and implementing effective management techniques. By gaining a comprehensive understanding of absenteeism and learning proactive approaches to manage it, HR professionals can foster a healthier, more engaged workforce that supports organizational goals.

## The Impact of Absenteeism on Productivity

Absenteeism can disrupt operations and lead to a chain reaction that affects an entire team or department. When employees are frequently absent, their responsibilities often fall to co-workers, increasing workloads and potentially leading to stress and burnout. This additional burden can diminish morale, reduce productivity, and create friction among team members who feel overworked or resentful.

As HR consultants, we are well aware that the financial costs of absenteeism are also significant.

Studies show that absenteeism costs businesses billions annually due to lost productivity, overtime payments for replacement workers, and potential delays in project timelines. In industries where shift work is common—such as healthcare, retail, and manufacturing—the immediate need for coverage can also lead to increased labour costs and administrative time in managing schedules. Furthermore, absenteeism can erode customer satisfaction when delays or reduced service quality affect clients.

# Identifying Root Causes of Absenteeism

To address absenteeism effectively, it's crucial to understand the underlying causes, which can vary widely among employees. Identifying these root causes allows HR professionals to implement targeted solutions that improve attendance and engagement. Common causes of absenteeism include:

## Health-Related Issues

Physical and mental health conditions are among the most prevalent causes of absenteeism. Chronic illnesses, injuries, and workplace-induced stress can lead employees to take frequent sick days. Mental health concerns, such as anxiety and depression, are increasingly recognized as significant contributors to absenteeism, with many employees struggling silently.

## Work-Life Balance Conflicts

Balancing work and personal responsibilities can be challenging, particularly for employees with caregiving duties or other personal commitments. Issues like childcare, eldercare, or other family obligations can cause employees to miss work unexpectedly. Work-life balance is a priority for many employees, and the inability to manage it effectively often results in increased absences.

## Work Environment and Culture

A toxic or unsupportive work environment can lead to disengagement, decreased job satisfaction, and higher absenteeism. Employees who feel undervalued, overburdened, or unsupported by management are more likely to take frequent days off, especially if they experience workplace bullying, favoritism, or other negative dynamics.

## Lack of Engagement or Motivation

Low morale and lack of engagement with one's role can result in a desire to avoid work. Employees who feel unfulfilled, unchallenged, or unrecognized in their positions may show up less frequently. Job satisfaction and motivation are often driven by a sense of purpose, and when employees lack this, they may view attendance as less critical.

## Burnout and Stress

Burnout, characterized by exhaustion, cynicism, and reduced professional efficacy, is a common issue that leads to absenteeism. Employees who experience high levels of stress—whether due to workload, unrealistic deadlines, or lack of control—are more likely to take sick days to recover. Addressing burnout requires a holistic approach, focusing on both workload management and providing support resources.

## Strategies to Improve Attendance

Now we know some of the main causes of absenteeism, let us look at some proven strategies to improve attendance. We begin with health and wellness programs.

## Implement Health and Wellness Programs

Some employers may see cost as a deterrent to implementing health and wellness programs in the workplace, but an economic decision requires a comparison of cost and benefit. In many cases, the benefits far outweigh the costs.

Offering comprehensive health and wellness programs can have a positive impact on employee attendance. Programs such as on-site health clinics, mental health resources, gym memberships, and wellness challenges encourage employees to take proactive steps toward their health. By promoting a healthy lifestyle and providing support for physical and mental well-being, organizations can significantly reduce absenteeism tied to health issues.

## Encourage Work-Life Balance

Providing employees with flexible work arrangements, such as remote work options, flexible hours, or compressed workweeks, can help them better balance personal and professional commitments. Flexibility in scheduling empowers employees to meet their obligations outside of work without compromising attendance. This approach is particularly effective in reducing unplanned absences and improving morale.

## Enhance Employee Engagement

Engaged employees are more likely to feel motivated to show up and contribute. HR can foster engagement by recognizing and rewarding employee achievements, offering opportunities for growth and development, and creating a work environment that values input and collaboration. Regular feedback sessions, team-building activities, and clear career progression pathways can make employees feel connected to their roles and the organization.

## Address Burnout Through Workload Management

Managers should work closely with HR to ensure that workloads are reasonable and deadlines are achievable. Encouraging regular breaks, enforcing time-off policies, and monitoring signs of burnout can prevent employees from becoming overwhelmed. Employee Assistance Programs (EAPs) can offer counseling and support, while managers can focus on effective delegation and setting clear, manageable goals for their teams.

## Promote a Positive Work Culture

Cultivating a culture that prioritizes respect, diversity, and inclusivity can have a profound impact on attendance. By fostering a supportive work environment where employees feel valued, HR can help reduce absenteeism related to workplace conflicts or dissatisfaction. Open communication channels, a zero-tolerance policy on bullying, and team-building activities all contribute to a positive work culture.

# Absence Management Policies and Procedures

Establishing clear, fair, and consistent policies for managing absences is essential for both reducing absenteeism and addressing it when it arises. Effective absence management involves setting expectations, monitoring attendance patterns, and creating avenues for employees to communicate their needs. The following policies and procedures will go a long way toward reducing absenteeism.

## Define Attendance Expectations

HR should create a clear attendance policy that outlines expectations, procedures for reporting absences, and potential consequences for excessive absenteeism. Employees should know what is considered acceptable and unacceptable absenteeism, as well as the steps to take when they need time off.

## Track and Analyze Attendance Data

HR can identify trends and potential issues early by tracking absenteeism rates and patterns. For example, frequent absences following holidays or on specific days of the week may indicate job dissatisfaction or stress-related issues. Analyzing data allows HR to take a proactive approach, reaching out to employees when concerning patterns emerge.

## Establish a Return-to-Work Process

A structured return-to-work process ensures that employees re-enter the workplace smoothly after extended absences. This process may involve a check-in meeting to discuss any accommodations needed, support resources, or changes in workload. Showing genuine care during this transition can boost employee morale and help prevent future absenteeism.

## Consider a Paid Time-Off (PTO) Policy

Some organizations have shifted to a Paid Time-Off (PTO) model, combining vacation, personal, and sick days into a single bank. PTO policies allow employees greater flexibility and control over their time, reducing the likelihood of unplanned absences. This approach also reduces the administrative burden of managing different leave types.

## Implement a Progressive Discipline Approach

When absenteeism becomes excessive, HR may need to implement a progressive discipline approach. This should be applied fairly and consistently, starting with a verbal warning, followed by written warnings, and potentially leading to termination if attendance issues persist. However, HR should focus on understanding underlying causes before moving to disciplinary action.

Absenteeism, while a common issue, can be effectively managed with a thoughtful, proactive approach that addresses its root causes. By understanding the reasons behind absenteeism and implementing supportive policies, HR professionals can foster a work environment that encourages regular attendance, promotes employee well-being, and drives organizational productivity. From enhancing employee engagement and promoting work-life balance to creating robust absence management policies, *Mastering HR Challenges* equips HR professionals with the tools they need to create a resilient, committed workforce. In doing so, absenteeism shifts from being a costly disruption to an area where HR can make a lasting, positive impact on both employees and the organization as a whole.

## Further Reading

https://haiilo.com/blog/absenteeism-workplace/

https://firstup.io/blog/what-is-absenteeism-in-the-workplace/#:~:text=What%20is%20absenteeism%20in%20the,and%20productivity%20of%20your%20workfo rce.

**Brown, Charles, and James Medoff.** *The Economics of Absenteeism.* Cambridge University Press, 1982.

**Vaughn, Helen, and Ben Willmott.** *Absenteeism: A Practical Guide to Understanding, Measuring, and Reducing Employee Absence.* Chartered Institute of Personnel and Development (CIPD), 2008.

# CHAPTER 2
# RECRUITMENT AND
# TALENT ACQUISITION

*Hiring people is an art, not a science, and resumes can't tell you whether someone will fit into a company's culture.* **– Howard Schultz**

When Midtown Marketing needed a new digital strategist, Clara, the hiring manager, set out to find someone with the right technical skills. After weeks of interviews, she met Tom, whose resume was impressive but whose personality was reserved. Clara hesitated, unsure if he would fit in with her team's outgoing culture. Still, something about his dedication stood out, so she decided to dig deeper.

In a follow-up interview, Clara asked Tom about his proudest project. His eyes lit up as he shared how he had independently revamped a struggling campaign, transforming it into one of his former employer's biggest successes. Clara realized that his quiet demeanor belied a deep commitment to his work and a drive to succeed that would benefit the team.

Clara decided to take a chance, hiring Tom not just for his skills but for his potential. Over time, he became the go-to strategist, winning over clients with his innovative ideas and quietly lifting the entire team's standards. Through this experience, Clara learned that in recruitment, sometimes the best hires aren't the flashiest, but those whose passion and determination are just waiting for the right opportunity to shine.

According to SmartRecruiters, recruitment refers to the process of identifying, attracting, interviewing, selecting, hiring and onboarding employees. In other words, it involves everything from the identification of a staffing need to filling it.

Recruitment and talent acquisition are among the most strategic functions within human resources. Finding, attracting, and hiring the right candidates directly affects an organization's ability to achieve its goals and remain competitive. A well-executed recruitment strategy builds a strong workforce, enhances the organization's culture, and sets the foundation for long-term growth. However, the process of recruitment has become increasingly complex in today's dynamic job market, requiring HR professionals to balance multiple factors, such as job market competitiveness, organizational branding, and a candidate's alignment with organizational culture and goals.

This chapter explores the essential elements of effective recruitment and talent acquisition, from creating compelling job descriptions to honing screening and interview techniques. We'll also examine how to attract top talent, especially in competitive markets, and the critical role of employer branding in recruitment success. A thoughtful and strategic approach to talent acquisition not only fills immediate staffing needs but also positions the organization as an employer of choice, capable of attracting high-caliber talent who drive performance and innovation.

# Effective Job Descriptions and Postings

The foundation of successful recruitment starts with a well-crafted job description. Effective job descriptions not only communicate essential information about the role but also act as marketing tools that attract the right candidates. A good job description balances clarity and appeal, accurately outlining the job responsibilities, required qualifications, and expectations while also highlighting the organization's unique benefits and culture.

## Defining Key Responsibilities and Expectations

The core of a job description lies in clearly defining the essential responsibilities and expectations of the position. Clarity in job roles allows candidates to gauge whether they possess the requisite skills and experience, helping to reduce mismatched applications. Responsibilities should be listed in a prioritized and concise format, offering candidates a clear understanding of their primary duties and the skills they will utilize in their roles.

## Outlining Necessary Qualifications and Skills

Listing the required qualifications and skills is another crucial component, as this informs candidates of the essential criteria for the role. HR should distinguish between required and preferred qualifications to avoid discouraging potentially suitable candidates who may not meet every single criterion but possess valuable skills. Including both hard and soft skills offers a comprehensive view of the ideal candidate profile, giving applicants a sense of the competencies valued by the organization.

## Showcasing Organizational Culture and Values

A job posting is an opportunity to communicate the organization's mission, values, and culture. Adding a few lines about the company's values, mission, and vision helps candidates understand the cultural fit, allowing them to determine if the organization aligns with their personal and professional goals. Emphasizing aspects like diversity, inclusivity, innovation, or community involvement attracts candidates who resonate with these values, improving the likelihood of long-term retention.

# Highlighting Growth Opportunities and Benefits

Mentioning professional development opportunities, potential career paths, and benefits like flexible work arrangements or health insurance makes the position more appealing. Today's candidates often seek growth opportunities and value perks beyond the paycheck, so highlighting such aspects in job postings can improve applicant quality.

## Optimizing for Search Engine Visibility and Accessibility

With the majority of job seekers using online platforms to search for roles, optimizing job descriptions with relevant keywords enhances visibility and accessibility. Using terms and phrases specific to the industry and position increases the likelihood of the job posting appearing in search results, widening the applicant pool. Accessibility considerations, such as clear formatting and a readable font size, also make postings more user-friendly, promoting inclusivity in the application process.

## Results-orientation Job Descriptions

The typical job description adopts a duty-oriented format. For example, a receptionist's job description might state that his or her role is to answer the telephone. In our experience, we have found that emphasizing results over duties proves to be more productive. Therefore, stating that the role of the receptionist is to help callers by answering the telephone enhances the receptionist's performance. Appendix 4 contains a sample results-oriented job description.

## Screening and Interview Techniques

Effective screening and interviewing processes are key to identifying candidates who not only have the qualifications but also align well with the organization's culture and values.

## Resume Screening and Application Review

Resume screening is the first step in the selection process. HR professionals should look beyond qualifications, focusing on skills, experience, and career progression. Technology can assist with this process, with many organizations employing Applicant Tracking Systems (ATS) to streamline resume screening by highlighting candidates whose resumes contain relevant keywords and skills.

## Phone Screening and Initial Assessment

Conducting a brief phone screening can be an effective way to gauge candidates' interest, confirm qualifications, and determine if they meet the basic criteria before scheduling an in-depth interview. A quick conversation about a candidate's background, interest in the role, and salary expectations allows HR to further refine the pool, saving time for both the organization and the applicant.

## Behavioural and Competency-Based Interviewing

Behavioural interviewing, which asks candidates to provide examples of past behaviour in specific situations, can be an effective way to predict future performance. Competency-based questions evaluate whether the candidate has demonstrated the necessary skills, such as problem-solving or teamwork, in previous roles. This method offers insights into how candidates handle challenges and interact within a team setting, giving a deeper understanding of their suitability.

## Situational and Technical Assessments

For roles requiring specific technical skills or decision-making abilities, situational or technical assessments can provide valuable insights into a candidate's capabilities. Simulating real-world scenarios allows candidates to showcase their skills in action, helping hiring managers evaluate their readiness for the role.

### Assessing Cultural Fit

While skills and experience are essential, cultural fit is equally important for long-term success and job satisfaction. Asking questions that reveal candidates' values, motivations, and preferred work environments allows HR to gauge alignment with the organization's culture. Engaging multiple interviewers can provide varied perspectives on whether the candidate will thrive within the company culture.

## Attracting Top Talent in Competitive Markets

In a competitive job market, organizations must adopt creative strategies to attract top talent. Today's job seekers often have multiple offers and are drawn to companies that provide compelling benefits, a strong workplace culture, and career development opportunities.

## Competitive Compensation and Benefits Packages

To attract top talent, organizations need to offer competitive compensation and benefits that stand out in the market. Transparent and fair salary ranges, combined with benefits like healthcare, retirement plans, and flexible working options, make positions more attractive. Offering unique perks, such as tuition assistance, mental health resources, or wellness programs, can further distinguish the organization from competitors.

## Creating a Positive Candidate Experience

The candidate experience, from initial contact through the onboarding process, significantly affects how job seekers perceive an organization. A seamless and respectful application process, prompt communication, and meaningful interactions create a positive impression that can increase the likelihood of candidates accepting offers. Every touchpoint, including interviews and follow-up communication, should reinforce the organization's commitment to a supportive and inclusive work environment.

## Utilizing Employee Referral Programs

Employee referrals can be one of the most effective methods of recruiting top talent. Employees who refer candidates are often incentivized, and referred candidates tend to perform better and have longer tenures. Leveraging referral programs can also reduce hiring time and costs, as referred candidates are often more familiar with the organization and culture through their connections.

## Expanding Recruiting Channels

To reach a diverse and qualified talent pool, organizations can expand their recruiting channels to include platforms like LinkedIn, industry-specific job boards, university partnerships, and social media. Casting a wide net allows companies to attract diverse candidates who bring unique perspectives, enhancing innovation and inclusivity within the workforce.

## Investing in Networking and Community Engagement

Attending industry events, hosting open houses, and engaging with local communities can build a pipeline of qualified candidates interested in working with the organization. Active engagement with the community and industry allows HR to create relationships with potential candidates, making recruitment efforts easier when positions open.

## The Role of Employer Branding

According to Workable, employer branding is the representation of a company as an employer. It's the image a company projects to attract and retain talent. This branding encompasses the company's values, work culture, and reputation in the job market.

Employer branding—the perception of an organization as an employer—plays a central role in recruitment. Candidates today seek more than just a paycheck; they want to work for organizations that align with their values, provide growth opportunities, and maintain a positive culture.

## Defining the Employer Value Proposition (EVP)

The Employer Value Proposition articulates what makes an organization unique and why it's a great place to work. A strong EVP highlights the benefits, opportunities, and values that set the organization apart, helping to attract talent whose career goals align with what the organization offers.

## Showcasing Organizational Culture

Candidates are drawn to companies with strong, positive cultures that value diversity, inclusivity, innovation, and work-life balance. Highlighting cultural initiatives, such as employee recognition programs or inclusivity efforts, helps HR demonstrate what it's like to work at the organization.

## Leveraging Employee Testimonials

Current employees are powerful advocates for an organization. Their testimonials, shared through the organization's website, social media, or recruitment materials, provide authentic insight into the work environment and daily life within the company. Employee stories and testimonials can resonate with candidates, offering a genuine look into the organization's culture.

## Consistency Across All Touchpoints

Employer branding should be consistent across all platforms, from job postings and websites to social media and networking events. Consistency reinforces the organization's message and strengthens the brand in the minds of potential candidates. Every interaction should reflect the values and culture that make the organization unique.

## Utilizing Digital Marketing and Social Media

Social media platforms like LinkedIn, Instagram, and Twitter allow companies to reach a broad audience of potential candidates. Digital marketing campaigns that highlight career paths, employee experiences, and corporate values showcase the company's commitment to its people. Active social media engagement can expand the talent pool and help HR build a reputation as an employer of choice.

Recruitment and talent acquisition are dynamic processes that require a strategic approach. Crafting compelling job descriptions, implementing rigorous screening and interview techniques, and focusing on employer branding are all critical to attracting and hiring top talent. In competitive job markets, organizations must go beyond traditional recruitment methods to create positive candidate experiences, highlight unique benefits, and ensure alignment between the organization's values and those of potential employees.

By mastering the complexities of recruitment and talent acquisition, organizations can build a workforce that drives growth, innovation, and resilience. As discussed in this chapter, the recruitment process is not just about filling vacancies—it is about finding individuals who will thrive in the company's environment and contribute meaningfully to its vision and goals. The importance of recruitment goes beyond simply hiring; it's about creating a workforce that embodies the organization's values, drives its mission, and sustains a positive work culture.

From defining the role and creating attractive job descriptions to implementing fair and effective screening practices, every step in the recruitment journey plays a role in establishing the organization as an employer of choice. In addition to competitive compensation and comprehensive benefits, today's top talent values authenticity, inclusivity, and growth opportunities. The more these values are emphasized in the recruitment process, the more effectively an organization can build a dedicated and loyal workforce.

Moreover, employer branding is not merely a marketing tactic; it is a reflection of the organization's values, priorities, and workplace culture. Investing in a strong employer brand fosters a positive perception, attracting candidates whose ambitions and principles align with the organization's vision. This alignment leads to greater job satisfaction, improved retention rates, and a cohesive workplace culture.

In the following chapters, we'll continue exploring the spectrum of human resources challenges, from retention strategies and performance management to fostering an inclusive culture and addressing evolving workforce needs. Each component of the HR function contributes to a thriving organization, and with a solid foundation in recruitment and talent acquisition, HR leaders are better equipped to drive success in other areas. By laying the groundwork with a thoughtful and strategic recruitment process, HR professionals can help shape an engaged, motivated, and future-ready workforce that supports the organization's objectives and propels it towards long-term success.

In sum, recruitment and talent acquisition are foundational pillars of organizational health. Investing in these processes brings not only immediate benefits but also lasting value as the organization evolves. As HR professionals continue to refine and enhance their approaches, they become powerful stewards of talent, steering the organization toward a future of growth, adaptability, and lasting impact.

## Further Reading

**Smart, Geoff and Randy Street.** *Who: A Method for Hiring.* Ballantine Books, 2008.

**Smart, Mark.** *Hiring for Attitude.* McGraw-Hill, 2016.

# CHAPTER 3
# EMPLOYEE RETENTION STRATEGIES

*Train people well enough so they can leave, treat them well enough so they don't want to.* - **Richard Branson**

Sophia had been with her company for nearly a decade. She started as a junior analyst and worked her way up to a senior management role. Over time, however, the long hours, lack of career development, and disconnection from company leadership wore her down. One day, she handed in her resignation. Her exit left a hole in the team that took months to fill, and by then, the company had already lost several more talented employees, costing time, money, and morale.

Sophia's story is a familiar one. Organizations often pour resources into attracting top talent but neglect the equally important task of retaining them. Employee retention isn't just about preventing turnover—it's about creating an environment where employees feel valued, motivated, and engaged for the long term. In this chapter, we'll explore why employees leave, and how to develop effective retention programs and strategies that keep top talent on board.

Employee retention is a critical concern for HR professionals in today's competitive job market. With the cost of turnover ranging from lost productivity to expensive recruitment efforts and a destabilized workforce, depending on who leaves, organizations cannot afford to lose good top talent. This chapter explores effective retention strategies that go beyond traditional perks and benefits, focusing on long-term employee engagement and satisfaction. By understanding why employees leave and developing proactive programs, HR professionals can create an environment that fosters loyalty, career growth, and a positive workplace culture. Retaining valuable employees not only reduces costs but also enhances organizational stability and growth.

# Why Employees Leave - Understanding Turnover

Employee turnover can be costly—not just in terms of recruitment expenses but also in the loss of organizational knowledge and team morale. But why do employees leave? Understanding the root causes of turnover is the first step toward building strong retention strategies. Common reasons include:

## Lack of Career Development

Employees often leave when they feel there's no room for growth or advancement. If individuals don't see a clear path forward, they're likely to seek opportunities elsewhere.

## Inadequate Compensation and Benefits

Financial compensation isn't everything, but when employees feel underpaid, it contributes significantly to job dissatisfaction.

## Work-Life Imbalance

Burnout is a major cause of turnover, particularly in industries with high workloads and long hours.

## Poor Management or Leadership

People often leave managers, not companies. Poor communication, feeling disrespected, micromanagement, or lack of recognition can drive employees away.

## Lack of Recognition and Feedback

Employees want to feel that their efforts are noticed and appreciated. Without regular feedback or acknowledgment, they may feel disengaged.

We cannot solve a problem if we don't understand the cause, so if your company is having a high turnover, as the HR gatekeeper, conduct an analysis to which of these issues could be the culprit. You might actually have to face the fire and find out from employees in which areas their dissatisfaction lies and then work as actively as you can to stop the leak by developing effective retention strategies.

## What is the cost of a high employee turnover?

Staff who are disengaged, bored, dissatisfied or are going downhill from the peak productivity curve are often **not** giving their best. Not only does this translate to the most obvious issue of lessened productivity, but it actually hampers their customer service delivery. And before you start thinking, "well it's okay if they are not forward-facing staff members", remember there are also internal customers – colleagues. Imagine staff member A waiting on information from another staff member B to complete his task and because staff member B is disgruntled, disengaged and actively job searching, he is not invested in meeting deadlines or giving his best which in turn affect the output of Staff A. As it relates to external customers, you can lose clients and sales if your staff member provides poor customer service. So your internal and external customers are affected and you know this is bad for business.

The cost of high employee turnover can be substantial, both financially and in terms of organizational health. Studies suggest that turnover-related expenses can account for 50% to 200% of an employee's salary, depending on the role. For example, the Society for Human Resource Management (SHRM) reports that the average cost per hire is around $4,000, with costs escalating when factoring in lost productivity, training new employees, and onboarding time. These hidden costs also include missed deadlines, reduced team morale, and the need for temporary workers or overtime to meet organizational needs. (

https://knowledge.wharton.upenn.edu/article/why-employee-turnover-costs-more-than-you-think/)

https://www.applauz.me/resources/costs-of-employee-turnover

In specific geographical areas, although specific turnover costs may vary, the situation mirrors global trends where high turnover can damage team cohesion and drive up recruitment and training costs. Employee turnover also impacts a company's reputation, making it harder to attract top talent. In a market where employee retention is crucial, addressing turnover helps foster a stable and productive workplace, directly affecting an organization's bottom line.

To avoid these pitfalls, organizations need robust retention strategies that focus on employee engagement, clear career development paths, and a supportive work culture.

## Developing Retention Programs

An Employee Assistance Program (EAP) counselor, once worked with a company that was experiencing a high turnover rate. Employees were frequently quitting, citing stress, lack of recognition, and minimal growth opportunities. One employee, let's call him Mark, reached out to her through the company's EAP, struggling with burnout. He loved his work but felt stuck, unnoticed by leadership, and saw no path forward in the organization.

Through their sessions, it became clear that his dissatisfaction wasn't just about workload—it was about a lack of connection and growth. He craved mentorship and felt like the older male managers were more focused on themselves than on grooming others. He also talked about his goals as a younger man joining the company and what he perceived as a lack of career advancement. Mark had even considered leaving for another company, which offered more visible growth opportunities. They talked though his issues and she asked him to draft a plan, based on his needs and the company's capacity, to see how they could create a win-win situation.

The counselor brought this feedback to the company's HR and management team, emphasizing the importance of professional development and employee recognition. They responded by implementing an internal mentoring program. They were not in a position to provide a career progression paths, but Mark felt heard, seen and the mentoring helped him to find other ways to grow. Over time, this change didn't just benefit Mark, but also improved morale as two others were also selected for mentoring.

By focusing on retention strategies like mentorship and recognition, the company was able to foster a more positive work culture and retain valuable talent. Mark, who had once felt like he had no future with the company, not only stayed but also took on a leadership role within his department when something opened up about eight months later. The benefit for the company was that it did not have to go outside to hire someone for the new position.

This shows that employee retention isn't just about pay or benefits. It's about understanding what makes people feel valued and giving them the tools to grow within the organization. Often, employees leave not because they dislike the work, but because they don't see a future with the company.

Effective retention programs are proactive, not reactive. Instead of trying to stop employees from leaving after they've decided to go, organizations should invest in strategies that keep them engaged from the start. Here are some key components:

***Employee Onboarding:*** A strong onboarding program helps new hires integrate into the company culture, understand their role, and feel valued from day one.

***Regular Employee Surveys:*** Use anonymous surveys to gather honest feedback about job satisfaction, management, and work conditions.

***Work-Life Balance Initiatives:*** Implement flexible scheduling when appropriate, remote work options, and mental health support and wellness programs to reduce burnout.

We also cannot trivialize the importance of the ***exit interview***. When employees do leave, conduct exit interviews to learn about any underlying issues. This information can be invaluable for improving retention strategies. A sample exit interview form is contained in Appendix 5.

> **The greatest asset of a company is its people. Retain them, and the company retains its success.**
> — Unknown

## The Importance of Career Development and Growth Opportunities

As we have mentioned, one of the most effective retention tools is offering employees clear opportunities for growth. Why? When employees see a future within the company, they are less likely to seek opportunities elsewhere. How? Here are some ways:

- Professional Development: Invest in employee training programs, workshops, and certifications to help employees enhance their skills.

- Mentorship Programs: Pairing employees with mentors can provide guidance and help them map out their career paths within the company.

- Internal Mobility: Encourage employees to explore different roles within the company by offering internal promotions and lateral movements.

- Performance Reviews: Regularly scheduled reviews that focus on both current performance and future goals help employees feel engaged and aligned with the company's direction.

- Career development isn't just about upward mobility; it's also about creating learning opportunities that keep employees challenged and engaged.

# Building a Positive Company Culture

Sometimes as an HR professional, you inherit certain problems when you come onboard a new organizational train – the company culture is one of them. A company's culture is its heartbeat. It defines how employees interact, feel about their work, and whether they see a future within the organization. Realistically, when you realize the culture is not ideal, it helps if you have the blessing of management, before you attempt to make changes. Also, don't move too fast too soon, because you know what they will say, "Oh so she is the new sheriff in town and wants to ride in and uproot what we are accustomed to"? As bad as the culture is, it is the nature of some employees, or some people to be resistant to change, so watch your timing. Positive workplace culture is built on several pillars.

First there is the matter of leadership transparency. Employees who feel they are "in the loop" are more likely to stay engaged. Regular communication from leadership about company goals and challenges brings about a sense of belonging. Employees being recognized and rewarded for their achievements is also a huge plus; this can be done at staff meeting, on bulletin boards or in the company newsletter. Inceptive programs are also helpful as tangible incentives. If your company is strapped for cash, see how you can offer swaps with other organizations.

Another key factor of the company culture is the matter of inclusion and diversity. Employees should feel welcome and accepted equally regardless of race, country of ori gin, sex, political persuasion, religion or other factors. A diverse and inclusive environment fosters creativity, innovation, and belonging, making employees more likely to stay. The organization must actively promote team-building activities to encourage collaboration and to build camaraderie; this helps to build relationships with the staff which can increase job satisfaction.

Employee retention is not about throwing money at the problem or offering superficial perks. It's about creating an environment where employees feel valued, supported, and see a future for themselves. By understanding why employees leave, offering growth opportunities, and fostering a positive workplace culture, HR professionals can build strong retention strategies that benefit both the employees and the organization as a whole. Retaining top talent isn't just a cost-saving strategy—it's the key to long-term success.

## Further Reading

**Dierdorff, Erich C., and Robert S. Rubin**, *The Retention Revolution: How to Keep Your Best Employees from Leaving.* McGraw-Hill Education, 2021.

**Kaye, Beverly, and Sharon Jordan-Evans**, *Love 'Em or Lose 'Em: Getting Good People to Stay.* Berrett-Koehler Publishers, 2018.

# CHAPTER 4
## MANAGING PERFORMANCE AND PRODUCTIVITY

*Productivity is never an accident. It is always the result of a commitment to excellence, intelligent planning, and focused effort. –* **Paul J. Meyer.**

Charles, a sales team leader, noticed that one of his team members, Sarah, had been struggling to meet her targets. She was talented and hardworking, but her confidence seemed to be slipping, and her productivity was taking a hit. Determined to help, Charles scheduled a one-on-one meeting to understand the issue.

In their conversation, Charles learned that Sarah felt overwhelmed by high expectations and feared she wasn't cut out for the role. Charles listened patiently and reminded her of her strengths—her persistence, her ability to connect with clients, and her previous successes. He then set up a plan to support her, breaking her goals down into manageable steps and offering weekly check-ins for guidance.

With Charles's encouragement and clear guidance, Sarah's confidence began to rebuild. Within a month, her numbers improved, and soon she was not only meeting her targets but exceeding them. This experience taught Charles that performance management isn't just about setting high standards— it's about providing support, feedback, and encouragement to help people reach their potential.

Vocabulary.com defines performance as follows:

*The act of doing something successfully; using knowledge as distinguished from merely possessing it.*

However, we would like to point out that performance is not always satisfactory or successful. In fact, unsatisfactory performance is one of the major workplace challenges identified by HR professionals. Closely related to performance is productivity which is defined by the Cambridge Dictionary as:

*The rate at which a company or country makes goods, usually judged in connection with the number of people and the amount of materials necessary to produce the goods.*

In any organization, employee performance and productivity are crucial indicators of success. Managing these elements effectively requires a careful balance between setting clear expectations, providing constructive feedback, and fostering an environment where employees feel empowered to excel. Human Resources (HR) professionals play a central role in this process by creating and implementing strategies that encourage optimal performance while addressing any challenges that may arise. This chapter explores practical approaches to managing performance and productivity, covering the essentials of setting expectations, conducting performance reviews, handling underperformance, and motivating high achievers.

# Setting Clear Expectations and Goals

Setting clear expectations and goals forms the foundation of any effective performance management system. When employees understand what is expected of them, they are better equipped to focus their efforts, prioritize tasks, and achieve objectives aligned with organizational goals. To ensure that expectations are meaningful and motivating:

## Align Individual Goals with Organizational Objectives

Each role within the organization should contribute to the broader goals of the organization. HR should collaborate with department heads and team leaders to design individual goals that align with these overarching objectives, making each employee aware of how his/her work fits into the company's vision.

## Use the SMART Framework

Clear, achievable goals are often set using what is typically referred to the SMART criteria:

**S**pecific

**M**easurable

**A**chievable

**R**elevant

**T**ime-bound.

By following this approach, employees gain a clear understanding of their targets, the standards by which they will be assessed, and the timeframe within which they need to deliver results.

## Provide Regular Updates and Adjust Goals as Necessary

Business conditions, market demands, and individual projects can change over time, requiring adjustments to employee goals. Regular check-ins between supervisors and employees offer a forum to update goals, clarify objectives, and address any potential roadblocks, ensuring that employees remain focused and aligned with evolving priorities.

## Performance Review Best Practices

Effective performance reviews are integral to managing productivity and ensuring ongoing employee development. Traditional annual reviews are increasingly supplemented by more frequent check-ins and feedback, which allow for timely adjustments and greater engagement. Key best practices for performance reviews include:

## Conduct Reviews Regularly

While annual reviews provide a broad overview, quarterly or even monthly reviews allow for more frequent feedback, helping employees course-correct quickly and maintaining engagement. These reviews can vary in formality, from structured meetings to more casual check-ins, depending on organizational culture and individual needs.

## Create a Two-Way Dialogue

A successful performance review should be a two-way conversation, providing space for employees to discuss their achievements, challenges, and aspirations. Encouraging feedback from employees can also provide valuable insights for HR on workplace dynamics, resource needs, or process improvements.

## Focus on Development

Performance reviews should go beyond assessing past performance; they should also be forward-looking, helping employees identify areas for growth and develop action plans to reach their goals. By providing resources such as training, mentorship, or additional project opportunities, HR can support employees in reaching their full potential.

## Address Bias and Ensure Fairness

HR should be vigilant about minimizing bias in performance evaluations. Standardized criteria, objective metrics, and 360-degree feedback—where input is gathered from supervisors, peers, and subordinates—are all methods that can contribute to a fairer assessment process.

# Addressing Underperformance

Underperformance is a challenge that requires a proactive, solution-focused approach. Identifying and addressing underperformance early on can prevent the issue from affecting team morale or productivity. Effective strategies for managing underperformance include:

## Identify the Root Cause

Before implementing corrective measures, HR and supervisors should identify the root cause of an employee's underperformance. Common factors include lack of training, unclear expectations, personal issues, or poor alignment between the employee's skills and job requirements.

## Create a Performance Improvement Plan (PIP)

A Performance Improvement Plan is a structured process that outlines specific areas of improvement, action steps, and a timeframe for assessment. The PIP should be developed collaboratively between HR, the supervisor, and the employee, clearly defining expectations and providing the necessary resources or training to support improvement.

## Offer Support and Resources

Addressing underperformance should focus on support, not punishment. HR can facilitate training, mentorship, or one-on-one coaching to help the employee develop the skills needed to meet expectations. A supportive environment fosters trust, allowing employees to make improvements without fear of punitive action.

## Follow Up and Evaluate Progress

Regular follow-ups ensure that the employee remains on track and feels supported throughout the improvement process. After the specified timeframe, HR should evaluate progress against the initial goals, making adjustments if necessary or proceeding with further action if improvement goals have not been met.

## Motivating High Achievers

High achievers are often self-motivated and ambitious, consistently exceeding expectations. However, if they feel underappreciated or lack opportunities for growth, they may become disengaged or seek new opportunities elsewhere. HR can foster high achievers' motivation through:

## Recognition and Rewards

Publicly acknowledging high achievers' contributions and offering tangible rewards can reinforce their motivation and drive. Rewards might include monetary bonuses, extra time off, or public recognition in team meetings. Additionally, personalized rewards—such as giving high achievers the chance to lead special projects—can be highly effective.

## Provide Opportunities for Growth

High achievers are often driven by a desire for growth and advancement. Offering them leadership training, mentoring, or challenging projects can keep them engaged and provide a pathway for career progression within the organization.

## Encourage Autonomy and Responsibility

High achievers often thrive when given more autonomy and responsibility. Allowing them greater control over their work can foster a sense of ownership and accountability, which can further drive their productivity and satisfaction.

## Involve Them in Decision-Making

Seeking input from high achievers on strategic decisions or involving them in goal-setting processes can increase their investment in the company's success. Engaging them in decision-making also shows that their perspectives are valued and trusted, enhancing their commitment to the organization.

Managing performance and productivity is a critical aspect of HR's role, one that impacts organizational success directly. By setting clear expectations, regularly evaluating progress, and providing targeted feedback, HR professionals can foster a culture of continuous improvement and accountability. Managing underperformance effectively ensures that all employees meet the standards required for success while motivating high achievers drives overall productivity and innovation. Each component of performance management contributes to building a workforce that is not only skilled but also deeply invested in the organization's vision and success.

The strategies discussed in this chapter provide a roadmap for managing performance, yet they are only part of a broader HR strategy. When implemented effectively, these strategies help create an environment where employees are supported, challenges are addressed proactively, and achievements are celebrated, ultimately resulting in a more engaged, productive, and resilient workforce. The chapters ahead will build on these concepts, exploring additional HR strategies to support talent development, foster inclusivity, and cultivate a thriving workplace culture that promotes both individual and organizational success.

## Further Reading

**Daniels, Aubrey C.** *Performance Management: Changing Behavior That Drives Organizational Effectiveness.* Performance Management Publications, 2016.

**Grote, Dick.** *The Performance Appraisal Question and Answer Book: A Survival Guide for Managers.* AMACOM, 2001.

**Pink, Daniel H.** *Drive: The Surprising Truth About What Motivates Us.* Riverhead Books, 2009.

# CHAPTER 5
## EMPLOYEE TRAINING AND DEVELOPMENT

*We now accept the fact that learning is a lifelong process of keeping abreast of change. And the most pressing task is to teach people how to learn.*

**– Peter Drucker**

No matter how much an employee knows when he or she is hired, there is always room for that employee to learn and to grow. Make no mistake about that!

Employee training and development plays a crucial role in the success of any organization. As HR professionals, it is your responsibility to ensure that employees are not only well-prepared for their current roles but also equipped with the skills needed for future challenges, especially when you keep succession planning and the organizational vision in mind. Effective training programs help with improved employee performance, boost motivation and engagement, foster innovation in the workplace, and help to build alignment with organizational goals.

Considering how organizations are evolving and how dynamic they are, continuous learning is not just a perk but a necessity. This chapter explores how to identify training needs, design impactful programs, and create a culture of learning through mentorship, coaching, and upskilling.

## Identifying Training Needs

Before designing any training program, the first step is identifying the actual training needs of the workforce. A sample Training Needs Assessment is found in Appendix 3. Here are some other ways to identify training needs:

1. Job descriptions – Knowing what is expected of the employees gives some insight into the knowledge and skills required of them. If an employee is hired with some of what is needed, but lacking the remainder, then that gap can be covered in training. The Job specification specifies the skills and abilities required to do the job.

2. Performance Evaluations – Regular performance reviews can reveal areas where employees need improvement or additional skills.

3. Skills Gap Analysis – This compares the skills your workforce currently has with what will be needed in the future, especially with the rapid advancement of technology and the direction in which the company wants to go.

4. Employee Feedback – Employees often can give some insight into where they feel underprepared. Surveys and focus groups can be effective in gathering this data.

5. Industry Trends – Monitoring industry changes can also help you stay ahead of the curve and prepare employees for upcoming demands.

Identifying training needs ensures that the time, resources, and efforts invested in employee development are both relevant and valuable to organizational goals.

## Designing Effective Learning Programs

After the training needs have been identified, the HR department then has the responsibility of designing effective learning programs. If the company is large enough, a training and development officer is a good investment and this will fall under that person's purview. The programs designed should be engaging, accessible, and tailored to the unique needs of both employees and the company. A key aspect of this process is customization based on the diverse learning styles of employees, and since people absorb information differently, it's essential to incorporate a blend of visual, auditory, reading, writing and hands-on approaches. This makes the learning experience more inclusive and ensures that employees can grasp the material in a way that resonates with them individually.

External trainers should be briefed on training guidelines, so even though the topics and styles are different, certain key factors and quality indicators should be upheld.

Setting clear objectives for each training program is another fundamental component. Each workshop/seminar/class should have specific, measurable goals that guide both the content delivery and the evaluation of the program's effectiveness. Clear objectives provide a roadmap for progress and help ensure that the training addresses the intended skill gaps or areas of development.

Here are some examples:

| Topic | Objective 1 | Objective 2 |
|---|---|---|
| **Diversity, Equity, and Inclusion (DEI) Training** Focuses on creating inclusive workplaces by addressing unconscious bias, cultural competence, and fostering equity for all employees. | Increase awareness and understanding of unconscious biases, microaggressions, and their impact on workplace dynamics. | Equip employees with tools and strategies to foster a more inclusive and equitable work environment, promoting collaboration and respect across diverse teams. |
| **Leadership Development** Aimed at building leadership skills among managers | Develop leadership skills in emotional intelligence, decision-making, | Enhance problem-solving and conflict-resolution abilities, enabling leaders to navigate |

| | | |
|---|---|---|
| and potential leaders. Topics often include emotional intelligence, conflict resolution, and decision-making. | and effective communication to improve team management and productivity | challenges and foster a positive work culture. |
| **Cybersecurity Awareness** Provides employees with knowledge about cyber threats, phishing scams, data protection, and safe online practices to safeguard company information. | Educate employees on identifying and mitigating common cybersecurity threats such as phishing, malware, and social engineering attacks. | Reinforce best practices for data protection, including password security, safe browsing, and the responsible handling of sensitive information. |
| **Employee Wellness and Mental Health** Training sessions promoting mental well-being, stress management, work-life balance, and the importance of self-care in high-stress environments. | Equip employees with strategies for managing stress and maintaining mental health, promoting a better work-life balance | Raise awareness of available wellness resources and support systems within the organization to foster a healthier and more supportive work environment. |
| **Communication Skills** Focuses on | Improve active listening and verbal | Develop techniques for providing and |

| improving interpersonal and professional communication, including active listening, conflict resolution, and effective team collaboration. | communication skills to enhance teamwork, collaboration, and conflict resolution in the workplace | receiving constructive feedback to foster professional growth and stronger relationships among employees. |
| --- | --- | --- |

Another thing, if you are new to HR and don't have a training specialist to identify what is needed for staff development, here is a brief sample of types of training you want to consider:

- Onboarding and orientation training
- Customer Service Training
- Sales Training
- Compliance Training
- Safety & Risk Management
- Technical Training
- Soft-Skills Training
- Diversity & Inclusion
- Leadership & Management
- Products Training

Obviously, the choice of the type of training will depend on the industry and the specific company.

## Making a Case for In-Person Training

Everything now is about technology... it is taking over the world and when used appropriately, is amazing. For example, technology is helping people who are visually impaired to achieve Ph. D studies. Truly, technology plays a significant role in enhancing the accessibility and flexibility of training programs. E-learning platforms offer employees the ability to access training materials from any location, making it particularly valuable in remote or hybrid work settings. This flexibility allows employees to engage with the content at their own pace and at times that are most convenient for them, thereby making it a convenient option.

However, in-person organizational training offers distinct advantages over hybrid or online methods, particularly when it comes to fostering engagement, building interpersonal connections, and providing hands-on learning experiences. Here's a case for why in-person training remains an effective option for companies looking to invest in their employees' development:

## 1. Enhanced Engagement and Focus

In-person training creates a more focused environment where distractions are minimized. Unlike virtual or hybrid sessions, employees are physically present, making it easier for trainers to maintain participants' attention. Face-to-face interaction also facilitates better engagement through real-time questions, discussions, and feedback, which can be harder to replicate in an online setting.

## 2. Stronger Interpersonal Connections

One of the key benefits of in-person training is the opportunity for employees to network and bond.

Building relationships through shared experiences, group discussions, and collaborative exercises promotes teamwork and camaraderie, which often leads to improved communication and cooperation back in the workplace. These interpersonal relationships can be difficult to replicate in a virtual setting where participants may feel disconnected from one another.

### 3. Immediate Feedback and Adaptability

In-person training allows facilitators to read the room, adjust pacing, and clarify concepts as needed. Participants can ask questions in real time and receive immediate feedback, making it easier to address misunderstandings or delve deeper into complex topics. In contrast, hybrid or online settings often face delays in communication or technical issues, hindering this seamless interaction.

### 4. Hands-On Learning and Practical Application

For certain types of training, particularly those that require hands-on practice (e.g., technical skills, safety protocols, or product training), in-person training is far more effective. Participants can engage in real-life simulations, role-playing, or equipment handling, which enhances their ability to apply what they've learned directly to their job functions. These activities are harder to replicate in an online format.

### 5. Encourages Participation and Accountability

Being in a physical setting encourages more active participation, as employees are less likely to multitask or disengage. The face-to-face nature of in-person training creates an environment of accountability, where participants feel more compelled to contribute to discussions and stay involved throughout the session.

*6. Building Organizational Culture*

In-person training also plays an essential role in fostering company culture. When employees gather in the same space, it reinforces the organization's values, mission, and community spirit. These shared experiences contribute to a stronger sense of belonging, which is harder to replicate in hybrid or online environments.

So while the financial controllers might support virtual training modes because it is cheaper, it is incumbent upon you as the HR professional to explain the cost/benefit ratio and explain why in-person is overall better for the employee and the organization.

***For sessions that have to be outsourced, ensure that the trainer has excellent communication skills, understands people engagement and classroom management, is adept at course design, and also understands learners' needs.***

# The Role of Mentorship and Coaching

Mentorship and coaching are powerful tools in employee development. They provide personalized guidance and feedback, helping employees to deal with challenges and grow in their roles. They also can be used reinforce learning concepts that cannot be taught in a classroom. ie. some employers may request telephone ettiquette however a staff member really needs to be coached on the nuances of sounding professional on the phone based on their voice, pitch or how they convey a professional message. It can also highlight deficiencies in supervisory practices. By coaching the supervisor, they may be able to effectively monitor and manage how the staff members are on the phone.

Mentorship – Pairs less experienced employees with seasoned professionals who can offer advice, share their experiences, and provide a broader perspective on career development. Mentorship programs help in talent retention, as employees feel more connected and supported within the organization.

Coaching – Unlike mentorship, which tends to be more relationship-based, coaching is typically more structured and goal-oriented. Professional coaches or trained managers help employees set performance goals and work on specific areas of development.

Both mentorship and coaching foster an environment of trust and open communication, which are critical in personal and professional development. Moreover, employees who feel supported in their growth are more likely to stay with the company long-term.

Employee training and development are key drivers of both individual and organizational success. By identifying training needs, designing relevant and engaging learning programs, fostering continuous development, and incorporating mentorship and coaching, organizations can build a skilled, adaptable, and motivated workforce. Investing in your employees not only improves their performance but also enhances job satisfaction, retention, and organizational loyalty. For HR professionals, creating a strong culture of learning is a crucial component of driving long-term success in any company.

## Further Reading

**Biech, Elaine.** *The Art and Science of Training,* Association for Talent Development (ATD) Press, 2017

**Noe, Raymond A.,** *Employee Training & Development.* McGraw-Hill Education, 2020

# CHAPTER 6
## DEALING WITH
## WORKPLACE CONFLICTS

*The Law of win/win says: Let's not do it your way or my way; let's do it the best way.* – **Greg Anderson**

It was a typical busy Monday morning when Sarah, the head of the marketing department, found an urgent email in her inbox. It was from John, the head of sales, expressing his frustration over missed deadlines and inadequate communication between their teams. He claimed that the marketing team had failed to deliver the required promotional material on time, causing delays in their sales campaign. Sarah, on the other hand, felt that John's team had not provided clear guidelines or sufficient time to create effective marketing content. Tension had been building up for weeks, and now, it was starting to affect the working relationship between both departments.

As the HR professional assigned to handle this issue, you understand that the conflict isn't just about missed deadlines or communication lapses. It's about different expectations, misunderstandings, and the lack of a clear, structured conflict resolution process. Without timely intervention, this tension could escalate, impacting team morale and overall productivity. This is a prime example of the type of workplace conflict that HR professionals deal with every day, and it's important to have strategies in place to address these situations effectively.

Workplace conflict is inevitable in any organization where all kinds of individuals with varying personalities, perspectives, and responsibilities interact. Conflict in and of itself does not have to be a bad thing as it can lead to the introduction of new ideas, drive problem-solving mindsets and help teams to become stronger. The problem comes when conflicts are not managed, but are left unresolved; they can escalate, negatively impacting workplace harmony, productivity, and overall organizational success.

For HR professionals, managing and resolving conflicts is a critical skill, as unresolved disputes can disrupt the flow of work and create a toxic work environment. In this chapter, we'll explore the common causes of workplace conflicts, strategies for resolution, and the importance of mediation and creating a harmonious work environment.

## Common Causes of Workplace Conflicts

Conflicts can arise in the workplace for a variety of reasons. While disagreements are a natural part of working with others, certain factors tend to trigger more intense and disruptive conflicts. These include:

## Poor Communication

Lack of clear directives, miscommunication, messages not properly delivered, unclear expectations, or inadequate information can lead to misunderstandings and friction among employees. Departments acting independently without sharing their plans, supervisors who don't speak to each other, and other such issues spell disaster.

## Personality Clashes

Staff are likely to have different working styles, preferences, and temperaments, which can sometimes result in personality conflicts. Interestingly, some people just do not take to each other for no obvious reason.

## Unfair Workload Distribution

Perceptions of unequal work distribution or persons getting less work or special overtime because of favoritism can spark resentment among employees.

## Resource Constraints:

Limited resources, such as time, tools, or personnel, can create competition and conflict, especially in high-pressure environments.

## Role Ambiguity

Unclear job roles and responsibilities often lead to confusion and frustration, resulting in disputes over who is accountable for certain tasks.

## Company Politics

Sometimes, persons are jealous when someone else gets a promotion, or a manager might appear to favour an employee, and these things can lead to tension and conflict. Actually, politics can also cause workplace conflict.

## Resistance to Change

Some staff members expect things to stay the same all the time and dig in their heels when there is a change. This can cause friction as others who have accepted the change can feel resentment to those who are lagging behind. When they joined the company, things were done one way and now they are being asked to do things differently and they don't want to.

## Conflicting values

Let's face it – people are different and have different value systems, which can cause a clash at work. Can you imagine an employee of a utility company who considers herself/himself to be a Christian and having to disconnect the electricity of a visually impaired elderly customer, and arguing about it with her/his boss? Or a sales clerk being asked to put damaged items at full price?

And the list goes on.... You have seen the issues that arise and know that this list is by no means exhaustive. Recognizing the root causes of conflict in your workplace is the first step toward effective conflict resolution.

## Preventing Conflict

Although we have acknowledged that in some instances, conflict can drive discussion, creativity and a broadened perspective, for the most part, when prolonged, it is unpleasant and can create a toxic environment and hamper the smooth flow of the work. We must therefore look at prevention.

Preventing workplace conflict involves fostering a positive environment and proactively addressing issues before they escalate. Here are several key strategies:

1. Clear Communication: Ensure clear, respectful, transparent, and consistent communication using the appropriate channels.

2. Set Clear Expectations: Clearly define roles, responsibilities, and expectations to minimize confusion and frustration. Ensure job descriptions are detailed and results-oriented.

3. Encourage Collaboration: Promote teamwork and interdepartmental collaboration, encouraging employees to work together towards common goals.

4. Provide Conflict Resolution Training: Equip employees and managers with conflict resolution and communication skills to address issues constructively.

5. Offer Regular Feedback: Provide constructive feedback regularly, so performance issues or misunderstandings are addressed early.

6. Establish Open-Door Policies: Create a culture where employees feel comfortable bringing up concerns or grievances before they become larger conflicts.

7. Promote Emotional Intelligence: Encourage self-awareness, empathy, and effective stress management among employees to handle tensions professionally.

8. Foster Inclusivity and Diversity: Embrace diverse perspectives and promote a culture of respect to prevent bias and discrimination-driven conflicts.

9. Implement Anti-Bullying Policies: Ensure there are strict policies against bullying and harassment, making it clear that such behavior will not be tolerated.

10. Address Problems Early: When a conflict arises, resolve it quickly before it escalates into a larger issue.

## Dealing with Special Issues

There are times when you will encounter certain employees displaying some specific issues that cause disruption in the organization. Sometimes their manager or supervisor feels unable to deal with them and so their behavior often runs unchecked. It is then your duty, however dreaded, to confront and deal with such employees. Let's examine some of these "special" issues.

### *Bullying*

An HR professional should handle workplace bullying with a zero-tolerance policy, ensuring swift intervention. This begins with confidentially investigating complaints and gathering evidence. The HR professional should facilitate mediation, when appropriate, to address the issue between the parties. Once there is sufficient evidence of bullying, disciplinary action should be taken to maintain a safe, respectful environment. Support systems like counseling should be offered to victims, and company-wide training on anti-bullying policies must be implemented to prevent recurrence.

### *Insubordination*

When managing insubordination, the HR professional should first investigate the root cause of the behavior, as among other things, it could stem from poor boundaries on the part of the senior person's side. The HR professional should conduct a formal meeting with the employee hearing his or her side of the story, outlining clear expectations and providing constructive feedback. If the behavior persists, a documented warning process or performance improvement plan (PIP) may be necessary. It's essential to also offer communication or leadership training to supervisors and managers to help them to help employees align with the company's culture and hierarchy.

## Gaslighting

Gaslighting involves subtle manipulation, making it critical for HR to intervene delicately yet decisively. The HR professional must gather evidence of manipulation and psychological abuse. Confidential discussions with both the victim and the accused party are essential. If gaslighting is confirmed, swift corrective measures—ranging from counseling to conflict management classes—should be implemented. Additionally, emotional intelligence training can foster a more empathetic workplace and prevent future occurrences of this toxic behavior.

## Passive-Aggressive Behavior

Passive-aggressive behavior can create a toxic atmosphere, undermining teamwork. An HR manager should confront this behavior by holding one-on-one conversations with the employee to address underlying issues. Offering coaching or counseling can help individuals manage frustration in healthier ways. Conflict resolution training and promoting direct, respectful communication can reduce passive-aggressiveness, ensuring smoother workplace interactions.

## *The Connected Employee*

It might so happen that employees feel that an employee with personal connections to upper management is not pulling his or her weight or is getting special treatment. This scenario requires extra care to avoid perceptions of favoritism. The HR manager must ensure that such an employee is held to the same standards as everyone else and if indeed the employee is taking advantage of his/her position, the employee must be reminded of his/her work contract or expectations. Transparency in decision-making, including disciplinary actions, is crucial to maintain fairness and equity. HR should promote a culture where all employees are valued based on merit, ensuring that the connected employee's relationship with management does not undermine team morale or productivity.

By addressing these behaviors with clear policies, effective communication, and the appropriate interventions, HR personnel can create a more harmonious and productive workplace.

## Conflict Resolution Strategies

Now let's get to the meat of the matter. How do we handle these workplace conflicts after the fact – employees are already not speaking, workflow is being affected, internal and external customer service has dropped, and people are sending in endless sick-leaves to avoid having to speak with or work with each other. Ladies and gentlemen, the bull has left the pen!!

Many of these are similar to the prevention techniques but the context is different as you are addressing something that is already a problem and trying your best to contain it before it erupts like a gigantic volcano. Here are some key strategies for resolving workplace disputes:

1. Address the conflict immediately: As soon as it is brought to your attention, conduct an investigation and start with listening to the parties directly involved.

2. Active Listening: It's really essential that you practice all your listening skills here. Pay attention to what is said and seek clarification. Ask questions for what was left unsaid. Focus on the facts and while feelings are important, for work related issues, it is not just about a person's perception of what was done but what is the evidence that it was done... get to the "nitty gritty" of things. It might seem time-consuming but you will probably save time getting it done right the first time. Ideally, you want an environment where individuals feel heard and understood.

3. Stay Neutral: As an HR professional, maintaining neutrality is vital. Avoid taking sides and focus on facilitating a constructive dialogue between the parties. Once employees are convinced you are not taking sides and they can expect fairness, they will tend to be more open.

4. Identify the source of the conflict. Is it a personality matter, a communication matter, an unclear policy matter, a timing issue? It's important to hone in on the

root cause of the conflict, so that you can construct appropriate target interventions.

5. Focus on solutions, not blame: Encourage employees to shift their focus from assigning blame to finding mutually agreeable solutions. This approach fosters collaboration rather than division and seeks a win-win solution. Recognize that employees seek solutions differently with some being avoiders, some competers, some collaborators, some compromisers and some accommodators.

6. Set a goal: Identify what is a common goal that persons involved in the conflict have. What would an ideal outcome look like? What would help; the organization, the specific department and the employees? For example, a department with communication issues might make a decision to have monthly meetings where information can be shared in all directions.

7. Evaluate: Always remember to check back in with the persons involved to evaluate the effectiveness of the interventions. Even if the problem is not solved, you can at least see if they are moving in the right direction.

Three things we want to emphasize here: (1) a reminder to ensure there are clear guidelines for acceptable behavior in the workplace, (2) ensure that all employees are aware of the procedures for conflict resolution and (3) documenting the information related to the conflict is of utmost importance.

# Mediation Techniques for HR Professionals

Mediation is a structured process whereby a third party sits with two feuding persons to attempt to bring about some form of resolution that leaves both parties satisfied. It is a powerful tool for resolving workplace conflicts. There are court-trained mediators who can be helpful, especially as being an external agent, employees would tend to think those persons are more objective. When an external person is not available, as an HR professional, you may be called upon to mediate between employees or teams to find a resolution. Here are some effective mediation techniques to consider as you take on this tricky role.

1. Facilitate Open Dialogue: Create a safe space where both parties can express their concerns without fear of judgment or retaliation. Make sure everyone has an equal opportunity to speak.

2. Identify Common Goals: Help both parties find common ground by identifying shared goals and values. This can foster cooperation and reduce hostility.

3. Encourage Compromise: Mediation often requires both parties to make concessions. Encourage them to compromise in ways that benefit both sides and the organization as a whole.

4. Follow Up: After mediation, follow up with both parties to ensure the conflict has been fully resolved and that any agreements reached are being honored.

# Fostering a Harmonious Work Environment

While resolving conflicts is essential, HR professionals should also focus on creating an environment that minimizes the likelihood of conflicts arising in the first place. This can be done by fostering a positive and inclusive company culture and includes all the techniques we have been discussing – promoting open communication with regular team meetings, have clear job descriptions, have occasional team-building activities to strengthen employee relationships, etc. The handbook should have clear guidelines on how conflict is handled and escalated.

Workplace conflicts are inevitable, but with the right strategies, HR professionals can address and resolve them effectively. By understanding the common causes of conflict, implementing effective resolution strategies, and fostering a positive work environment, organizations can minimize the negative impact of disputes and maintain a productive, harmonious workplace. Remember, the goal is not to eliminate all conflict but to manage it in a way that promotes growth, understanding, and collaboration.

# Further Reading

**Liddle, David.** *Managing Conflict: A Practical Guide to Resolution in the Workplace*, Kogan Page, 2017

**Shaw, Gerald.** *7 Winning Conflict Resolution Techniques*, Independently Published, 2018.

# CHAPTER 7
# DIVERSITY, EQUITY, AND INCLUSION (DEI)

*It is not our differences that divide us. It is our inability to recognize, accept, and celebrate those differences.*
— **Audre Lorde**

**Diversity:** *Differences among people with respect to age, class, ethnicity, gender, race, sexual orientation, personality traits, and other human differences.*

**Equity:** *The quality of being fair or impartial.*

**Inclusion:** *The practice or policy of providing equal access to opportunities and resources for people who might otherwise be excluded or marginalized.*

Do you fit into any of these categories?

- Women
- Black
- Migrant
- LGBTI
- Non-dominant religion
- Any other usually marginalized community

If so, you might have one time or another felt sidelined, spoken over, ignored, bullied, the butt of jokes, or some other action that caused you to feel uncomfortable. These and similar situations have pushed the need for conversations about diversity, equity and inclusion (DEI) in the modern workplace.

The Cambridge Dictionary defines DEI as: *"the idea that all people should have equal rights and treatment and be welcomed and included, so that they do not experience any disadvantage because of belonging to a particular group, and that each person should be given the same opportunities as others according to their needs."*

Diversity, Equity, and Inclusion (DEI) are essential to creating a workplace that values and respects all employees. A focus on DEI ensures that organizations don't just tolerate differences but celebrate them, promoting fair opportunities for growth, representation, and belonging. In today's increasingly diverse world, organizations should embrace DEI not just for ethical reasons, but also because there are tangible business benefits.

Paul, a man identifying as gay, was asked when using a male bathroom, if he is in the right place.

Susan, A female pilot was told she can't leave the cockpit to deal with menstrual cramps.

A female politician was told to "stop behaving aggressive like a man".

For all these real-life scenarios, the organizations had to have a serious talk with the persons making the comments and also implement DEI programs to foster understanding and inclusivity in the workplaces.

## The Business Case for DEI

Embracing diversity, equity, and inclusion is not just a moral imperative—it's actually good for business. Numerous studies (which we won't bother to quote) show that diverse teams perform better, demonstrate more innovation, and are more adaptable. Organizations that prioritize DEI see higher levels of employee engagement and retention – because everyone feels welcome and a sense of belonging. Who does not want to truly feel like a member of the team? Additionally, another aspect of embracing DEI is that companies that reflect the diversity of their customers are better positioned to meet varied market needs. How is that not a win? When people walk into a company and see someone who looks like them or sounds like them, they feel more comfortable.

Consider a medium-sized retail company that started deliberately recruiting employees from diverse cultural backgrounds to serve their equally diverse clientele and also started paying attention to what they sold. Not only did this help the company offer culturally sensitive products and services, but it also increased customer satisfaction and revenue. DEI initiatives can transform an organization's ability to reach new markets and respond effectively to a broader customer base.

## Promoting an Inclusive Culture

Angela, a woman of color in an executive role at an insurance company, noticed that when she spoke in meetings, she was often not acknowledged and her male colleagues often dominated the conversation. At first, she thought she was being sensitive, but she kept making efforts to speak up more and still felt alienated. As the only woman in top management, she felt ignored. She reported this to the HR manager, who then proceeded to conduct an unconscious bias training for senior leaders. She chose this route, because while some persons might not have been open to change, at least it was important for everyone to know what the company stood for. It actually helped to create awareness of communication and exclusive patterns that persons were not even overly conscious of exhibiting. Through open dialogue, the company was able to create a more inclusive culture where everyone's ideas were valued equally, significantly improving team dynamics and innovation.

Promoting inclusion means making sure that all employees feel valued and heard. It's about creating an environment where everyone, regardless of background, feels he/she belongs. Hiring practices are important, not as a tokenism measure, but using an Equal Opportunity framework. An Equal Opportunity employer is one that does not discriminate against employees based on their race, colour, religion, age, disability, or country of origin. However, we must note that inclusivity goes beyond hiring diverse employees; it's about ensuring they thrive within the organization. This requires proactive measures to dismantle stereotypes and unconscious bias.

Fostering and promoting an inclusive culture at your workplace can be done through the following ways:

> Encouraging open communication and dialogue about DEI. Something that is discussed openly has more of a change of thriving than a topic that is just spoken of in hushed tones behind closed doors.

> Conducting regular DEI training sessions. These sessions serve to educate staff about best practices and also clarify company policies, etc. Perple have the opportunity to role play scenarios and understand the importance of practice and compliance

> Creating policies to address breaches if someone is openly discriminating against others. Staff need to know what the evidence of such a breach looks like, so there is clarity.

> Celebrating cultural diversity with events, talks, and heritage months.

## Overcoming Bias in Recruitment and Promotion

Question: If you are hiring someone for the receptionist position in your company, do you make an effort to ensure the person is good-looking without stating that implicitly on the advertisement for the position? Is that wrong or right? Is it biased? What about another candidate who is not as aesthetically pleasing but has excellent customer service skills? What chance does that person have? Maybe there is no right answer, but at least you can see where we are going with the discussion.

We cannot begin to tell you about some of the complaints we get when we go into organizations to conduct training. Quite often, as it relates to hiring, the reports are that, it is done based on politics, who you know, favoritsm and other factors. Employees in certain positions have also complained of feeling like ageism and sexism are very rampant in some industries. One of the biggest challenges in achieving equity in the workplace is overcoming bias in recruitment and promotions. Unconscious bias can prevent qualified candidates from being considered for positions or advancement, often without the decision-makers even realizing it. We need to check ourselves to see how we are thinking. Do we automatically assume a man would be better as a pilot, or a woman would be better as a secretary? It would help if we were more open-minded about positions and focus on the skills, not the sex, the last name, the school the person attended but purely, "Is this human being the best fit for this job"?

Three things to consider to avoid hiring bias are:

1. Start with diversity goals in mind. Look at the data that shows the company diversity breakdown and make an effort to ensure that recruits are firstly, most suitable for the job, but also diverse.

2. Using work sample tests. Ask Candidates to complete tasks that are similar to the actual work they will have to do and see how they perform; this way they can be judged objectively on how they perform, rather than appearance.

3. Use standardized interviews. Ask all candidates the same questions and use a scorecard to rate answers objectively. This helps to reduce bias and focus on relevant skills.

When it comes to promotions, transparency is key. Employees should understand the criteria for advancement, and leadership should ensure that all employees, regardless of their background, are given equal opportunities for professional growth.

In a utility company, Deborah, a female engineer, felt that she was being overlooked for promotions compared to her male colleagues with similar qualifications. After consulting HR, the company established a standardized promotion review process, which helped eliminate favoritism and bias. Within a year, Deborah received a well-deserved promotion, improving morale and demonstrating the firm's commitment to equity.

## Implementing DEI Policies and Programs

Earlier, we mentioned the implementation of DEI policies and programs. This requires a deliberate and strategic approach. Organizations should assess their current DEI efforts, identify gaps, and create a plan that aligns with their values and goals. Effective DEI policies cover recruitment, promotion, compensation, leadership development, and employee retention.

Key steps for HR managers to implement DEI include:

- Creating a DEI committee to oversee efforts and measure progress

- Setting measurable goals related to hiring, retention, and promotion of diverse candidates

- Establishing mentorship programs that provide guidance and support to underrepresented groups

- Offering flexible work arrangements to accommodate diverse needs (e.g., for parents, people with disabilities, etc.)

- Regularly surveying employees to understand their sense of belonging and areas for improvement

Leadership involvement is crucial in ensuring that DEI policies don't remain on paper only, but are actively implemented and supported throughout the organization. HR professionals must work closely with leadership teams to integrate DEI into the company's core values and everyday operations.

Diversity, Equity, and Inclusion are not optional add-ons in today's workforce—they are essential for fostering a thriving, innovative, and productive environment. By implementing DEI strategies, HR professionals not only enhance employee satisfaction and retention but also contribute to the overall success of the business. By actively promoting an inclusive culture, addressing bias in recruitment and promotions, and crafting well-thought-out policies, organizations can cultivate a workplace where everyone, regardless of background, has the opportunity to succeed.

DEI is an ongoing journey, not a one-time effort. HR professionals have a vital role in shaping workplaces where diversity is celebrated, equity is maintained, and inclusion is lived out daily.

## Further Reading

**Johnson, Allan G.** *Privilege, Power, and Difference.* McGraw-Hill Education, 2017.

**Sue, Derald Wing.** *Race Talk and the Conspiracy of Silence: Understanding and Facilitating Difficult Dialogues on Race.* Wiley, 2015.

# CHAPTER 8
# EMPLOYEE HEALTH
# AND WELLNESS

*When "I" is replaced by "We", even illness becomes wellness.* – **Malcolm X**

*Employee wellness programs aren't a one-size-fits-all solution; they should be thoughtfully designed to support employees as individuals, addressing diverse needs to create an environment where everyone can thrive.* — **Arianna Huffington**

Many employers expect employees to come to work, focus on work and deal with their health issues outside of the job. It is reasonable for employers to expect employees to give 8 hours work for pay and to be in tip top shape while doing so, but the reality is that, things don't always go that way. Employees are human and deal with work and personal stress, environmental issues and even the workplace itself can have myriads of issues that affect employee wellbeing. In recent years, organizations have increasingly recognized the role of employee health and wellness programs in fostering productivity, improving workplace morale, and reducing healthcare costs. HR professionals now consider these programs essential components of effective employee engagement and retention strategies. This chapter provides HR leaders with insights into the benefits of employee wellness programs, best practices for design, strategies for managing stress, and ways to support a work-life balance.

## The Importance of Physical and Mental Health in the Workplace

While we are all aware that employers have a legal right to ensure a safe and healthy workplace, employee well-being goes beyond just that and actually encompasses both physical and mental health. When staff are physically and mentally well, this directly impacts performance and productivity, job satisfaction, and overall organizational health. Healthy employees generally report higher productivity, lower absenteeism, and reduced healthcare costs for the company. Mental health, equally important, contributes to a resilient and motivated workforce, decreasing turnover and the risks associated with burnout.

Data from the World Health Organization (WHO) and the Centers for Disease Control and Prevention (CDC) indicate that nearly one in five adults experience mental health issues in a given year. When organizations invest in physical and mental health resources, they support employees' comprehensive wellness and benefit from a more cohesive, productive, and engaged team.

## Physical Health

Work wellness programs that promote physical health through exercise initiatives, nutrition plans, smoking cessation programs and preventive healthcare can lead to better energy levels, improved concentration, a stronger immune response, and increased resilience. Care should also be taken to ensure that the workspaces are environmentally safe for employees and depending on the work, things like driving long hours, operating heavy duty equipment, working in excess heat or cold, noise and other factors should be taken into consideration. The CDC reports that physically active employees take fewer sick days and have lower healthcare costs, underlining the importance of physical wellness in reducing absenteeism and overall health expenses. They are able to focus better, can handle certain rigours of the job, and good physical health can also mean the employees can manage their tasks better.

## Mental Health

Mental health initiatives are equally important, aiming to reduce stress, anxiety, and depression in the workplace. Some of the work issues affecting employee mental health could be long hours, bullying, discrimination, high stress jobs, difficult managers, tight deadlines and heavy workloads. The workplace culture is of utmost importance as that can become toxic, making it a space where employees do not thrive, but just tolerate, until they can be someplace else. If these issues can be reduced or eliminated, then staff can be better adjusted and happier.

Happier staff work better together and are nicer to customers. Research from Harvard Business Review reveals that companies with robust mental health programs report up to a 30% reduction in absenteeism and increased employee engagement, underscoring the impact of mental health on workplace dynamics. Staff who are mentally well are able to be more creative; they can focus on solving work related issues and their performance is better.

Therefore, when seeking to sell the benefits of work wellness programs, here are some concrete benefits:

- Financial savings – reduced healthcare costs, reduced absenteeism, reduced need for temp workers to fill in when others are on sick leave.

- Increased productivity & performance – more consistent energy levels, better focus, better teamwork, better culture and environment.

- Lower turnover – increased job satisfaction, employees feel valued and supported and that causes an increase in loyalty.

# Designing Effective Wellness Initiatives

Designing a wellness program requires a comprehensive approach tailored to the unique needs of an organization. HR professionals can introduce resources such as Employee Assistance Programs (EAPs), counseling services, or mental health workshops. Programs must address physical and mental health and be adaptable, inclusive, and accessible. Steps that can be taken are:

## 1. Assess Employees' Needs and Preferences

To create a program that resonates with employees, HR should assess what employees' needs are – give them a say. This can be done when conducting employee appraisals, or through surveys or focus groups. Understanding employee preferences ensures higher participation and allows HR to develop wellness programs that truly support employees.

## 2. Set Clear Goals and Metrics

Setting measurable objectives helps monitor program effectiveness. Metrics could include employee participation rates – attendance at health events, health outcomes, and qualitative feedback. Establishing goals like reducing sick leave, improving morale, or enhancing mental health can guide HR in refining the wellness program over time.

## 3. Offer a Diverse Range of Wellness Options

A one-size-fits-all approach rarely succeeds. Offering various options—such as discounts for gym memberships, exercise or meditation sessions, or nutrition counseling—accommodates employees' diverse preferences and fosters broader participation. Recently, we offered men's health month sessions for some workplaces which included vitals (blood pressure, blood sugar and cholesterol checks), massages, talks from a urologist, spiritual leader and a nutritionist with a variety of handouts on men's issues and the men were very pleased to see this initiative and felt happy that they were the focus of these sessions. They were well received at all the establishments with men

## 4. Integrate Technology

The integration of wellness apps and digital platforms has made wellness programs more accessible. Apps like Calm for mindfulness or MyFitnessPal for tracking exercise and diet allow employees to engage with wellness on their terms, wherever and whenever is convenient. It is more convenient for some persons to access certain wellness information outside of work time. We also have a subscription program at https://www.consultkoren.com/eaphome where managers and staff on the program have access to articles, questionnaires, videos, infographics and a host of tools to help them.

## 5. Adjust Programs Based on Industry Trends and Current Issues

If your employees are health care workers during a pandemic or weather reporters in hurricane season, special attention must be given to these issues to ensure their wellbeing. For example, having shorter shifts. Also, if your measuring data show an uptick in stress-related issues (think accountant at end of year or during audits), then additional mental health support might be needed. It is also useful to observe health periods like prostate and breast cancer awareness, etc.

## 6. Encourage Regular Check-Ins and Updates

Regular evaluations ensure the wellness program remains relevant. Survey and forms feedback can help HR assess which components are working well and which need improvement and to gauge satisfaction levels, identify underused or ineffective resources, helping to align the program with evolving employee needs. In some instances, anonymous feedback can help as it encourages more honest responses. Managers also play a key role in assessing individual and team wellness needs, as they often have a clearer view of employees' daily stressors and challenges. Empowering managers to conduct informal wellness check-ins with their team members can help identify wellness needs early. This can also contribute to building a supportive, wellness-focused culture within departments.

Performing a comprehensive review of the wellness program annually allows HR to make larger, strategic adjustments. This review can be based on aggregated survey results, participation trends, and emerging wellness challenges, ensuring that program resources—whether digital health tools, in-person fitness programs, or counseling support—remain relevant and high-quality. We also have to remember that different life stages bring unique wellness needs. For example, younger employees may prefer fitness and stress management activities, while older employees may focus more on chronic disease management and financial wellness. Regular feedback enables HR to adapt the wellness program, catering to a diverse workforce with a range of wellness priorities.

## Managing Workplace Stress and Burnout

There is good stress like someone receiving a promotion and there is bad stress like someone else feeling he or she was more suited for the job so she gives the employee receiving the promotion a really hard time. The negative stress is a pervasive challenge in modern workplaces, and burnout—a state of chronic physical and mental exhaustion—can lead to serious repercussions, some of which we mentioned before and which includes apathy, increased absenteeism, reduced productivity, workplace conflicts and a huge financial cost to the organization. Addressing stress requires a multi-faceted approach that addresses the root causes.

**Encourage Open Communication.** Encourage a workplace culture where employees feel comfortable discussing stressors and mental health crises when needed. Train management to recognize early the signs of stress and promote regular dialogue between HR or management and staff to alleviate tension and provide a supportive environment.

**Consider Flexible Working Options.** Depending on the industry and type of position, flexible work hours and remote work options have, in some instances, helped to reduce stress. This flexibility helps employees manage work and personal responsibilities better, leading to reduced stress levels and improved job satisfaction. It's worthwhile to test these alternative measures to see how they work, before making them a long-term arrangement.

**Encourage Staff to use Vacation.** When staff use their annual vacation, they are better rested. In some companies, there are policies that only some days can be carried over to the next year.

**Demonstrate Compassion and Empathy.** When leaders show genuine understanding for employee challenges, that behavior fosters trust which increases employee engagement. The compassionate leader can seek solutions by adjusting workload or getting help for the employee to alleviate pressure, so stress does not become burnout.

Signs of employee burnout can be irritability, tension or conflict with other staff, increased sensitivity and constant complaining about everything.

# Encouraging Work-Life Balance

Work-life balance has been thrown around so much, it seems like we talk about it more than we actually practice it. It is fundamental to employee satisfaction and overall well-being. When employees feel they can manage work and personal life, they tend to be more engaged, productive, and committed to their roles. How do we encourage it?

• Promote Clear Boundaries

Encouraging employees to maintain clear boundaries between work and personal life can help them feel more balanced. HR can establish policies limiting after-hours communication and supporting "unplugged" time.

• Encourage Paid Time Off (PTO)

Promoting the use of PTO helps prevent burnout and contributes to work-life balance. Studies show that employees who take regular breaks feel more energized and demonstrate increased productivity upon their return.

• Offer Family-Friendly Policies:

Policies that support families, such as parental leave or flexible hours, help employees balance work with family responsibilities. These policies demonstrate a commitment to employee well-being and improve long-term retention.

• Educate Staff on Time Management Techniques:

Providing training on time management skills empowers employees to be more efficient, helping them allocate time for personal and professional responsibilities effectively.

Employee health and wellness programs are essential investments in an organization's most valuable asset— its people. These programs contribute to productivity, morale, and organizational culture, benefiting employees and employers alike. HR professionals play a crucial role in designing and implementing these initiatives, ensuring they are inclusive, adaptable, and impactful. Prioritizing employee well-being fosters a healthier, more engaged workforce and sets the foundation for a successful, forward-thinking organization.

## Further Reading

**Berry, Leonard L., Ann M. Mirabito, & William B. Baun**. *What's the Hard Return on Employee Wellness Programs?* Harvard Business Review, 2010.

**Goetzel, Ron Z., & Ronald J. Ozminkowski.** *The Health and Cost Benefits of Work Site Health-Promotion Programs. Annual Review of Public Health,* 29, 2008.

# CHAPTER 9
## COMPLIANCE WITH LAWS AND REGULATIONS

*Most businesses believe regulators intend to fine them rather than help them protect their workers. Serious violations should bring real consequences, but minor violations should only incur warnings that encourage compliance.* – **James Lankford**

When a new data protection law went into effect, Rachel, the HR manager at a mid-sized tech company, knew her team would need to adapt quickly. The regulation required more stringent handling of personal data, and Rachel was aware that even a small mistake could result in hefty fines and damage the company's reputation. She arranged a series of training sessions to help employees understand the new requirements, but some team members focused on their own deadlines, and brushed off the importance of compliance

One day, a project manager, James, accidentally shared a client's private data in an email chain.

Though no harm came of it, Rachel used this as a teachable moment, explaining how easy it was to overlook compliance details under pressure. She worked with James and the team to develop simpler, automated data-protection measures and emphasized a culture of diligence in handling sensitive information.

Thanks to Rachel's proactive and supportive approach, the team soon became fully compliant with the new law, implementing best practices that made everyone feel more secure. Rachel's response showed her team that compliance isn't just a legal burden—it's a shared responsibility to protect clients and the company, one thoughtful action at a time.

In today's complex workplace environment, compliance with laws and regulations is a fundamental aspect of Human Resources (HR) management. Organizations must understand and enforce an intricate landscape of labour laws, employment standards, anti-discrimination policies, and health and safety requirements, among others. These regulations are essential not only to protect employee rights but also to safeguard companies from legal risks, financial penalties, and damage to reputation. This chapter examines the importance of HR's role in ensuring compliance, exploring the various legal standards and guidelines that govern employment. By understanding the legal landscape, HR professionals can create policies, implement training, and develop systems that reduce risk and support fair, transparent, and legally compliant workplaces.

## Understanding Labour Laws and Regulations

Labour laws are designed to establish standards that protect both employees and employers by defining rights, obligations, and limitations within the workplace. These laws vary across regions, but common themes include the protection of workers' rights, regulation of wages, working hours, and workplace safety.

## Employment Laws

Employment laws operate at multiple levels, depending on the county to which they apply. Understanding these laws is crucial for HR to ensure full compliance.

## Anti-Discrimination and Equal Opportunity Laws

Anti-discrimination laws and regulations are in place to prevent bias based on race, gender, age, religion, and other protected characteristics. HR must be vigilant in creating an inclusive environment and applying these laws in hiring, promotions, terminations, and everyday workplace practices.

## Health and Safety Regulations

Health and safety regulations, often enforced by governmental bodies, are critical to ensuring safe working conditions. These regulations include guidelines on the use of protective equipment, incident reporting, and the management of potential workplace hazards. HR departments work closely with safety officers and other departments to ensure compliance, conduct training, and address potential safety concerns.

## Data Privacy and Employee Information Protection

Data privacy laws set standards for managing employee data and protecting personal information. HR professionals must implement data protection practices, ensuring that employee records, health information, and other sensitive data are securely managed and protected against unauthorized access.

## Ensuring Compliance with Employment Standards

Employment standards define the terms and conditions of employment, including wages, hours, overtime, and leave entitlements. HR plays a critical role in ensuring that these standards are met, which contributes to a fair and equitable workplace.

### Wage and Hour Compliance

Compliance with wage and hour laws is crucial to avoid legal risks and ensure fair treatment of employees. HR should track employees' working hours accurately, account for overtime, and ensure that employees are compensated according to relevant minimum wage laws.

### Leave Entitlements

Employees are entitled to various types of leave, including sick leave, vacation time, family leave, and other statutory leaves. HR departments need to manage these entitlements accurately, ensuring that employees can access their leaves in accordance with company policy and legal requirements.

## Youth Employment and Other Special Considerations

Employment standards often include provisions for youth employment, defining acceptable hours and conditions for minors. HR must also be mindful of any laws related to specific types of employees, such as those working in hazardous environments or pregnant employees, to maintain compliance and uphold safety standards.

## The Role of HR in Preventing Legal Risks

The proactive role of HR in preventing legal risks is essential for protecting the organization's reputation and financial stability. From establishing sound policies to providing training, HR departments are integral to reducing the likelihood of legal issues.

## Policy Development and Implementation

Clear, well-defined policies serve as a foundation for compliance. HR is responsible for developing, implementing, and communicating these policies, ensuring they align with current laws and regulations. These policies should cover a wide range of topics, including anti-discrimination, harassment prevention, workplace safety, and confidentiality.

## Regular Training and Education

Regular training sessions for employees and managers are essential to reinforce compliance and educate staff on relevant laws and organizational policies. This training can include anti-harassment workshops, data protection best practices, and safety training, all of which contribute to a culture of awareness and responsibility.

## Documentation and Record-Keeping

Accurate documentation and record-keeping are critical components of compliance. HR must maintain detailed records of employment contracts, payroll information, performance evaluations, disciplinary actions, and employee complaints. This documentation not only demonstrates compliance in case of audits or legal disputes but also helps HR identify potential issues early.

## Staying Updated on Legal Changes

Laws and regulations frequently change, and HR departments must stay informed to adapt their policies accordingly. HR professionals can keep up to date by attending seminars, joining professional HR associations, and consulting with legal counsel when needed.

## Conducting Internal Investigations

Internal investigations are necessary when allegations of misconduct, discrimination, or harassment arise. HR must handle these situations with integrity, confidentiality, and adherence to procedural standards to ensure fairness and minimize legal risks.

## Establish a Clear Process for Investigations

HR should establish a standardized process for handling investigations. This process typically includes steps such as fact-finding, interviewing involved parties, gathering evidence, and evaluating findings objectively. A well-defined procedure helps HR manage cases fairly and consistently, reducing potential legal challenges.

## Maintain Confidentiality and Impartiality

Maintaining confidentiality is essential during investigations to protect the privacy of all parties involved. HR should ensure that information is shared on a need-to-know basis and take precautions to prevent retaliation against individuals who report issues.

## Document Findings and Follow Through with Actions

HR should document the entire investigation process, including findings, conclusions, and any actions taken. Once the investigation is concluded, HR may need to implement corrective measures, which could range from employee training to disciplinary actions, to address the issue and prevent future occurrences.

## Follow Legal Standards for Fair Treatment

Internal investigations must be conducted fairly, without bias or preconceived judgments. HR should follow legal standards and internal policies to ensure that all employees are treated equitably, regardless of their role in the complaint.

Compliance with labour laws and regulations is a critical function of HR, essential to maintaining a fair, productive, and legally sound workplace. HR professionals are the stewards of compliance, tasked with understanding and applying the complexities of labour laws, developing policies, training staff, and ensuring thorough documentation. Proactively addressing compliance not only protects the organization from legal risks but also fosters a culture of trust, safety, and accountability among employees. By remaining vigilant and adaptable, HR can effectively manage compliance challenges, safeguarding both the organization's interests and the rights of its workforce. As we continue in this book, the following chapters will expand on related HR responsibilities, highlighting tools and strategies to strengthen compliance and legal adherence within various organizational frameworks.

## Further Reading

**Walsh, David J.** *Employment Law for Human Resource Practice.* Cengage Learning, 2020.

**Oppenheimer, Amy and Craig Pratt.** *Investigating Workplace Harassment: How to Be Fair, Thorough, and Legal.* Society for Human Resource Management, 2020

# CHAPTER 10
## COMPENSATIONS AND BENEFITS MANAGEMENT

*If you pick the right people and give them the opportunity to spread their wings and put compensation as a carrier behind it you almost don't have to manage them. –* **Jack Welch**

When the company's annual employee survey showed a drop  in morale, particularly around compensation, Maria, the HR director, knew she needed to dig deeper. Although the company offered competitive salaries, the feedback revealed employees felt undervalued and unsupported in areas beyond pay.

Maria took action by revisiting the benefits package. She introduced a flexible work-from-home policy, enhanced the wellness program with gym reimbursements, and added mental health support. She also created a small recognition fund, encouraging managers to reward employees with gift cards and personal notes for exceptional work.

After the changes, the atmosphere shifted. Employees felt their well-being and contributions were recognized, and productivity rose. Maria's response taught her team that compensation management isn't only about the numbers—it's about creating a workplace where employees feel valued, supported, and motivated to grow.

Compensation and benefits management is a critical aspect of Human Resources (HR) that has far-reaching implications for talent attraction, employee retention, and overall organizational success. The right mix of competitive salaries, comprehensive benefits, and additional rewards plays a significant role in meeting employees' financial needs, enhancing job satisfaction, and motivating productivity. As the labour market becomes increasingly competitive, companies need to craft compensation and benefits programs that set them apart, balancing financial incentives with meaningful, non-monetary rewards. This chapter explores best practices for structuring compensation packages, designing attractive benefits programs, ensuring pay equity, and using a range of rewards to recognize employee contributions.

## What is Compensation?

We adopt the definition of compensation offered by Sage:

*In the workplace, compensation is what is earned by employees. It includes salary or wages in addition to commission and any incentives or perks that come with the given employee's position.*

According to an *Indeed* survey, the vast majority of job seekers (83%) said good pay/compensation is the factor that most attracts them to a new job. Not only that, but 39% of workers said they are searching for a new job because they want better compensation or benefits. Clearly, compensation is an extremely important issue.

# Structuring Competitive Compensation Packages

An effective compensation package offers employees a fair wage for their work while aligning with industry standards and organizational budget constraints. Creating such packages involves thorough market research, consideration of various compensation models, and an understanding of the workforce's unique needs.

## Market Analysis and Benchmarking

Conducting market analysis helps HR determine competitive pay rates within specific industries, geographic locations, and job functions. Organizations can use salary surveys and benchmarking tools to compare their pay scales to those of competitors. This ensures that the compensation offered is competitive enough to attract high-quality candidates while retaining current employees. Regular reviews of market data are also essential, as compensation standards evolve based on economic conditions and job market shifts.

## Salary Ranges and Bands

Defining salary ranges and bands helps establish a structured approach to compensation that accommodates employees at different experience levels and job roles. Creating pay bands also provides clarity for career progression and internal promotions. Entry-level positions may have narrower pay bands, while roles requiring specialized skills often allow for broader salary ranges to accommodate varied expertise levels.

## Direct and Indirect Compensation

Compensation packages typically consist of direct (base salary, bonuses) and indirect (benefits, retirement contributions) compensation. Direct compensation is the core of most packages, providing the basic financial incentives for work. Indirect compensation adds significant value, covering health insurance, retirement plans, and other essential benefits that contribute to overall job satisfaction.

## Cost of Living and Regional Adjustments

Adjusting salaries based on geographic location is common in organizations with a distributed workforce. Cost-of-living variations necessitate these adjustments to ensure that employees receive fair compensation based on the expenses in their region. By integrating these adjustments, companies create equity across different locations, contributing to overall employee satisfaction.

# Designing Benefits Programs that Attract and Retain Talent

In addition to salary, benefits programs are a significant factor in both attracting and retaining top talent. Employees today seek packages that offer security, flexibility, and comprehensive coverage, which makes benefits design a critical function of HR.

## Healthcare and Wellness Programs

Health insurance is a cornerstone of any benefits package, with many companies now expanding coverage to include dental, vision, and mental health services. Beyond traditional healthcare, wellness programs that encourage physical and mental well-being, such as gym memberships or counseling services, are increasingly popular. These programs demonstrate a company's investment in its employees' overall health and well-being.

## Retirement and Financial Planning

Retirement benefits are essential for employees planning for long-term financial security. Additionally, some companies offer financial planning resources to help employees manage debt, savings, and investments. These benefits demonstrate a commitment to employees' future, fostering loyalty and reducing turnover.

## Flexible Work Arrangements and Paid Time Off

Flexibility in work arrangements has become highly sought after, particularly post-pandemic. Options such as remote work, flexible hours, and compressed workweeks are attractive incentives. Generous paid time off policies, including vacation, sick leave, parental leave, and personal days, also support work-life balance and contribute to a positive work environment.

## Educational and Professional Development Support

Supporting employees' professional growth by offering tuition assistance, certification reimbursement, or access to courses and workshops can be highly appealing. This not only builds employee loyalty but also helps upskill the workforce, ultimately benefiting the company as well.

## Pay Equity and Transparency

As awareness of pay disparities grows, pay equity has become a priority for many organizations. Addressing and ensuring equitable pay practices is not only a legal and ethical requirement but also vital for maintaining trust and fairness within the workforce.

## Conducting Pay Equity Audits

Regular pay equity audits help organizations identify potential disparities in compensation. These audits involve analyzing salary data across gender, race, and job functions to uncover discrepancies. Addressing these issues fosters a culture of fairness, where employees are rewarded equitably based on their roles, experience, and contributions rather than on demographic characteristics.

## Developing Transparent Pay Policies

Transparency in compensation policies promotes trust between employees and management. When employees understand the criteria for raises, bonuses, and salary bands, they are more likely to feel valued and motivated. HR can work with leadership to develop clear, accessible policies and guidelines that outline compensation structures, raise eligibility, and promotion paths.

## Legal Compliance in Pay Equity

Adhering to equal pay laws is essential to avoid legal complications and penalties. Ensuring compliance requires HR to keep updated on laws regarding pay equity, conduct internal audits, and address any identified pay gaps in a timely manner.

## Incentives, Bonuses, and Non-monetary Rewards

Beyond base salary and benefits, incentives and rewards can further enhance job satisfaction, recognize achievements, and motivate high performance. Structuring effective reward systems involves understanding employee needs and balancing financial and non-financial incentives.

### Performance-Based Bonuses and Profit Sharing

Performance bonuses are often tied to achieving specific goals, milestones, or productivity targets. Profit-sharing programs allow employees to receive a portion of the company's profits, creating a sense of ownership and alignment with the company's success. When employees feel that their efforts directly impact their financial rewards, it fosters a sense of pride and motivation.

## Recognition Programs and Non-Monetary Rewards

Recognition is a powerful motivator, often as impactful as financial incentives. Employee-of-the-Month awards, public acknowledgments in meetings, or celebrating project completions are simple yet effective ways to acknowledge employees' hard work. Non-monetary rewards like extra vacation days, gift cards, or even the option to choose certain assignments provide personal value beyond pay.

### Customized Rewards and Flexible Options

Personalized rewards that cater to employees' interests or needs can have a meaningful impact. Offering flexible benefits, such as allowing employees to select the rewards they value most, can increase job satisfaction. HR can provide options like childcare subsidies, wellness stipends, or travel vouchers, making rewards more relevant and attractive to diverse employees.

## Incentives for Long-Term Commitment

Retaining experienced and skilled employees is crucial for organizational stability and growth. Long-term incentives, such as stock options or sabbaticals, encourage employees to invest in the company and stay with it for the long term. By aligning employee interests with the company's growth, these incentives support sustained engagement and loyalty.

Effective compensation and benefits management requires a balanced approach that incorporates competitive salaries, attractive benefits, equitable pay practices, and meaningful rewards. Through strategic planning, HR can craft compensation programs that meet employee needs while supporting organizational goals. Compensation is more than just a paycheck; it reflects the organization's commitment to its workforce, influencing employee satisfaction, productivity, and retention. By focusing on both financial and non-financial aspects of rewards, companies can cultivate a work environment where employees feel valued, motivated, and committed. In an evolving workplace, adaptability and continuous improvement in compensation and benefits management will be key to maintaining a thriving workforce.

## Further Reading

**Berger, Lance A. and Dorothy R. Berger,** *The Compensation Handbook: A State-of-the-Art Guide to Compensation Strategy and Design.* McGraw-Hill, 2015.

**Martocchio, Joseph J.** *Strategic Compensation: A Human Resource Management Approach.* Pearson, 2020.

# CHAPTER 11
## LEADERSHIP DEVELOPMENT AND SUCCESSION PLANNING

*I'll bet most of the companies that are in life-or-death battles got into that kind of trouble because they didn't pay enough attention to developing their leaders.*
**– Wayne Calloway**


At Cedar Manufacturing, the leadership team recognized a growing need for effective succession planning. While the company had strong managers, many lacked formal leadership training, and with a wave of retirements on the horizon, the company faced uncertainty. Determined to address this issue, Suzan, the HR manager, initiated a leadership development program aimed at identifying and nurturing future leaders within the organization.

She started by surveying employees to identify those with potential and interest in leadership roles. Suzan then paired these high-potential employees with seasoned mentors and designed a comprehensive training curriculum that included workshops, real-world projects, and feedback sessions.

Among the participants was Mark, a mid-level supervisor with great potential but little confidence. Through the program, he learned to embrace his leadership style and gained the skills needed to inspire his team. After several months, Mark not only led a successful project but also contributed innovative ideas that improved processes across departments.

As the program progressed, the company saw a noticeable shift in its culture. Employees felt more engaged, and the pipeline of qualified leaders grew stronger. Suzan's initiative demonstrated that investing in leadership development is not just about filling positions—it's about fostering a culture of growth and preparing the organization for future challenges.

We begin our discussion by defining leadership development. Following PeopleHum, we define leadership development as follows:

*Leadership development is the process of enhancing an individual's ability to perform in a leadership role within an organisation. Leadership roles are those that help an organization's strategy be carried out by fostering alignment, gaining mindshare, and developing the talents of others.*

Effective leadership is essential to the sustainability and success of any organization. As companies deal with constant changes in technology, market demands, and workforce expectations, having a strong pipeline of leaders who can adapt and guide their teams becomes crucial. Leadership development and succession planning are essential components in building this pipeline, ensuring that organizations are not only prepared for inevitable transitions but are also equipped with leaders who embody the values, vision, and goals of the organization.

Leadership development involves identifying high-potential employees, fostering their competencies, and preparing them to take on greater responsibilities. Succession planning, on the other hand, is a proactive approach to identifying and grooming individuals for key roles, minimizing disruption during leadership changes. This chapter explores the steps for identifying potential leaders, the importance of building key competencies, creating a succession plan for critical roles, and the indispensable role HR plays in leadership development.

# Identifying Potential Leaders

One of the primary challenges in leadership development is accurately identifying individuals with leadership potential. Potential leaders are not only those who excel in their current roles but also possess qualities that indicate they can effectively guide teams and contribute strategically to the organization.

## Assessing Competencies and Soft Skills

Leadership potential goes beyond technical skills. Traits like emotional intelligence, adaptability, resilience, and strong communication skills are key indicators of leadership potential. Employees who demonstrate these qualities, especially in challenging situations, may be good candidates for leadership development. Assessments, personality tests, and 360-degree feedback can help identify individuals who exhibit these traits.

## Analyzing Past Performance and Growth

While past performance is not the sole indicator of future leadership potential, employees who have consistently met or exceeded performance expectations are often good candidates for advancement. Evaluating growth in their role, initiative-taking, and the ability to learn and improve over time are important indicators. Leaders are often those who show continuous progress, regardless of challenges.

### Incorporating Feedback from Multiple Sources

Gathering feedback from supervisors, peers, and even direct reports can provide a comprehensive picture of an individual's capabilities. High-potential leaders are often seen as dependable team players who inspire trust and respect. By integrating feedback from various sources, HR can make more informed decisions about potential leaders.

### Observing Initiative and Problem-Solving Skills

Potential leaders often display a proactive approach to problem-solving, seek solutions independently, and show initiative in tackling new challenges. This tendency to lead by example, take ownership of their work, and volunteer for challenging projects is often a sign of future leadership capability.

# Building Leadership Competencies

Once potential leaders have been identified, the next step is to foster the specific competencies they'll need to succeed in leadership roles. Leadership competencies can be divided into interpersonal, cognitive, and functional areas that support the responsibilities of a leadership position.

## Developing Interpersonal Skills

Effective leaders are adept at communication, empathy, and conflict resolution. These skills are critical for motivating teams, managing conflicts, and fostering collaboration. Leadership development programs should focus on refining these interpersonal skills through mentorship, training, and opportunities to lead team initiatives.

## Encouraging Strategic Thinking and Vision

Leaders must be able to see the big picture and anticipate future trends. Developing strategic thinking skills involves encouraging high-potential employees to participate in decision-making, analyze data, and think long-term. Workshops on strategic planning, competitive analysis, and critical thinking exercises can enhance these skills.

## Instilling a Focus on Results and Accountability

Successful leaders are results-driven and hold themselves and their teams accountable. Building this competency involves teaching potential leaders how to set clear goals, monitor performance, and measure success. Training on project management, metrics tracking, and performance evaluation fosters an accountability mindset.

## Enhancing Adaptability and Resilience

The business landscape is constantly changing, and adaptability is a must for leaders. Building resilience and adaptability requires exposing potential leaders to dynamic environments where they must adapt quickly. Rotational programs, project-based assignments, and scenario-based learning can prepare leaders to handle ambiguity and change.

## Creating a Succession Plan for Key Roles

A succession plan is a strategy for identifying and developing future leaders in an organization, not just for leadership positions, but for senior roles at all levels.

Succession planning ensures that organizations have a prepared and capable workforce to fill critical roles when vacancies occur. This process involves identifying key roles, developing internal talent to fill these roles, and creating a roadmap for smooth transitions.

## Identifying Key Positions and Their Requirements

Not all roles require a formal succession plan, so identifying critical positions that have a significant impact on the organization's success is essential. These are often executive or senior management roles, as well as positions requiring specialized knowledge. Once identified, a detailed profile outlining the required competencies, skills, and experience for each key position should be created.

## Evaluating and Preparing Successors

Succession planning isn't just about identifying successors; it's about preparing them for the roles within the organization. Potential successors should have access to mentorship and training tailored to the requirements of the positions they're being prepared for. This could include shadowing current role incumbents, participating in strategic planning sessions, and working on cross-functional projects.

## Implementing Cross-Training and Knowledge Transfer

Knowledge transfer is vital in preparing future leaders

for seamless transitions. Cross-training allows potential successors to develop a comprehensive understanding of the operations, responsibilities, and challenges associated with a position. Structured knowledge-sharing programs, documentation of procedures, and job rotation are all effective methods for ensuring a smooth knowledge transfer.

## Reviewing and Updating the Succession Plan Regularly

Succession planning is a dynamic process that requires regular reviews. Employees may leave, change career paths, or develop skills at different paces. Therefore, the plan must be flexible and updated periodically to reflect these changes and ensure it meets the organization's evolving needs.

## The Role of HR in Leadership Development

Human Resources plays an instrumental role in the development and implementation of leadership programs, guiding employees from potential to readiness for leadership roles. HR's role includes:

Facilitating training

Managing mentorship

Promoting an appropriate culture

Evaluating outcomes

### Facilitating Training and Development Programs

HR is responsible for creating, coordinating, and evaluating leadership training programs. These can include in-house workshops, external training, e-learning modules, or executive education. HR also ensures that training aligns with the organization's goals, equipping future leaders with the skills necessary to drive the company forward.

### Managing Mentorship and Coaching Initiatives

Mentorship is an invaluable tool in leadership development, and HR often facilitates these programs. Matching potential leaders with mentors or coaches allows for direct knowledge transfer, career advice, and personal development guidance. HR can also monitor these mentorship relationships, ensuring they meet both mentors' and mentees' expectations.

## Promoting a Culture of Continuous Improvement

HR fosters a culture where employees are encouraged to pursue personal and professional growth. This culture motivates potential leaders to continuously improve, participate in training opportunities, and seek feedback. By promoting continuous learning, HR contributes to an engaged and development-focused workforce.

### Evaluating Leadership Development Outcomes

HR plays a critical role in assessing the effectiveness of leadership programs. Metrics such as promotion rates, employee retention, and leadership effectiveness are used to gauge the success of these initiatives. HR's role in ongoing evaluation and adjustment ensures that the programs remain relevant and impactful.

Leadership development and succession planning are integral to building a resilient organization equipped to face future challenges. Identifying high-potential employees, cultivating their leadership skills, and creating succession plans for critical roles contribute to sustainable growth and continuity. As a central player in these processes, HR supports the organization's stability and ensures a steady pipeline of capable leaders who embody its values and objectives. When managed effectively, leadership development and succession planning not only protect against disruption but also promote a culture of growth, innovation, and excellence.

## Further Reading

**Charan, Ram, Stephen Drotter, and James Noel.** *The Leadership Pipeline: How to Build the Leadership Powered Company.* Jossey-Bass, 2011.

**James, Elijah M.** *The Leadership GPS: Guiding Your Team to Excellence.* EJ Publishing, 2024.

**James, Elijah M, and Koren Norton.** *Effective Succession Planning: The Key to Business Longevity,* 2022.

**London, Manuel.** *Leadership Development: Paths to Self-insight and Professional Growth.* Routledge, 2014

# CHAPTER 12
## MANAGING REMOTE AND HYBRID WORKFORCES

*People are more productive working at home than people would have expected. Some people thought that everything was just going to fall apart, and it hasn't. And a lot of people are actually saying that they're more productive now.* – **Mark Zuckerberg,**

When the pandemic hit, TechSol quickly transitioned to a remote work model. While most employees adapted well, Emma, a team leader, noticed that some team members struggled with the isolation and disconnection that remote work often brought. Particularly affected was Leroy , a talented programmer who had always thrived on collaboration and in-person brainstorming sessions.

Recognizing the impact on team morale and productivity, Emma decided to take action. She initiated weekly virtual team check-ins, not just for project updates but also for casual catch-ups, where everyone could share personal wins, hobbies, and even pet stories. Emma also encouraged "virtual coffee breaks" for smaller groups to foster connections outside of work-related discussions.

As the weeks passed, Leroy began to open up during these informal gatherings, sharing ideas and engaging more with his colleagues. The sense of camaraderie blossomed, and productivity soared. Emma's thoughtful approach to managing her remote team illustrated that even in a virtual environment, creating a strong, connected team culture is essential. By bridging the distance with empathy and intentional communication, she transformed challenges into opportunities for growth and collaboration.

The rise of digital technology and the need for workplace flexibility have driven a rapid transformation in traditional work models, giving way to remote and hybrid workforces. While initially prompted by the COVID-19 pandemic, the adoption of these models has endured and, for many organizations, become permanent. Remote and hybrid work models offer employees increased autonomy and work-life balance, while organizations benefit from a wider talent pool and often reduced operational costs. However, they also present distinct challenges: maintaining productivity, fostering collaboration, ensuring equitable access to resources, and navigating complex legal considerations.

In this chapter, we explore the multifaceted aspects of managing remote and hybrid workforces, addressing the challenges and opportunities unique to these models, best practices for maintaining productivity, strategies for effective communication, and the critical legal considerations involved. As remote work becomes integral to organizational strategy, HR's role in creating cohesive, productive, and legally compliant remote and hybrid teams has never been more essential.

OfficeRnD makes the following distinction between remote work and hybrid work:

*Hybrid work and remote work are not the same. Hybrid work combines elements of both in-office and remote work, allowing flexibility in where and when employees work. In contrast, remote work refers exclusively to working outside of a traditional office environment, typically from home or any other remote location.*

# The Shift to Remote Work: Challenges and Opportunities

The transition to remote and hybrid work has redefined the traditional concept of the workplace. This shift has allowed organizations to tap into global talent, reduce office space costs, and offer employees more flexibility. However, it also introduces challenges, especially in areas such as team cohesion, employee oversight, and maintaining organizational culture.

## Benefits of Remote Work

Remote work offers several advantages for both employers and employees. For companies, it broadens access to a diverse pool of talent, often improving workforce diversity and inclusivity. Additionally, remote work reduces the need for large office spaces, resulting in cost savings. Employees experience improved work-life balance, decreased commute times, and increased job satisfaction. These benefits contribute to greater employee retention and a more agile workforce capable of responding quickly to changes.

## Challenges of Remote Work

Despite the advantages, remote work presents challenges that require a shift in management strategies. Maintaining employee engagement, preventing isolation, and ensuring consistent communication are ongoing concerns. Additionally, managing performance without physical oversight requires managers to establish new forms of accountability and trust. For hybrid teams, equitable treatment between remote and in-office employees is critical to preventing divisions within the team.

## Opportunities for Improvement and Innovation

Remote work models also open the door for innovation. Organizations are developing creative solutions for virtual collaboration, such as video conferencing, project management tools, and communication platforms. Remote work has encouraged HR departments to rethink traditional policies and devise new methods for managing productivity, performance, and engagement in a virtual setting.

## Ensuring Productivity in Remote Settings

A key aspect of managing remote workforces is establishing practices that promote productivity and accountability without constant supervision. Productivity in a remote setting can be optimized through the following means:

- Clear goal-setting
- Performance monitoring
- Supporting self-discipline and work-life balance

## Setting Clear Goals and Expectations

To ensure productivity, it's essential to establish clear and measurable goals for remote employees. Goal-setting frameworks such as SMART (Specific, Measurable, Achievable, Relevant, Time-bound) goals are particularly effective for remote teams. By defining precise deliverables and timelines, managers can create accountability without needing to micromanage. Regular check-ins and progress reviews help keep employees aligned and motivated.

## Utilizing Technology for Performance Monitoring

Leveraging productivity tools such as project management software, time-tracking apps, and collaborative platforms helps monitor performance and workflow. These tools allow managers to track progress and identify bottlenecks while giving employees the autonomy to manage their time effectively. However, excessive monitoring should be avoided, as it can create a culture of mistrust that may hinder productivity.

## Supporting Work-Life Balance

Remote work often blurs the boundaries between personal and professional life, leading to risks of burnout. HR should promote work-life balance by establishing guidelines that respect personal time, such as setting limits on after-hours emails and encouraging employees to take regular breaks. Additionally, promoting the use of digital wellness programs and resources can help employees maintain their mental and physical health, fostering a more productive workforce.

## Fostering Collaboration and Communication in Hybrid Teams

In hybrid work models, where some employees work remotely and others are in the office, collaboration and communication can become complex. Maintaining a sense of unity and seamless communication requires intentional strategies and a mix of digital tools to bridge the physical divide.

### Creating Inclusive Communication Practices

Hybrid teams benefit from standardized communication practices that ensure equal participation. To prevent in-office employees from having an informational advantage, meetings should be conducted in ways that provide equitable access, such as hosting all meetings virtually even when some team members are in the office. Organizations can also implement communication policies that promote transparency and accessibility.

## Leveraging Collaboration Tools

Effective collaboration tools are essential for hybrid teams. Video conferencing, real-time messaging platforms, and collaborative software allow team members to connect and share ideas regardless of location. Encouraging the use of platforms such as Slack, Microsoft Teams, or Asana fosters open communication and provides a central location for shared resources, promoting cohesion among dispersed team members.

## Encouraging Team Bonding and Social Interaction

Maintaining team cohesion requires creating opportunities for remote and in-office employees to bond and interact socially. Virtual team-building activities, regular video check-ins, and company-wide virtual events can strengthen relationships and reduce the sense of isolation for remote employees. By fostering a sense of belonging, HR can help remote and hybrid teams feel more connected to the organization and each other.

## Ensuring Fair Treatment and Access to Resources

Hybrid models can unintentionally create disparities between remote and in-office employees in terms of visibility and access to resources. HR should work to ensure that both remote and in-office employees have equal access to information, support, and opportunities. This can involve offering stipends for home office equipment, conducting regular feedback surveys, and ensuring that remote employees have equal access to career development programs.

## Legal Considerations for Remote Workers

The legal landscape for remote and hybrid workforces is evolving, with new regulations and requirements emerging to address the unique circumstances of remote work. Ensuring compliance with these laws is critical for minimizing risks and protecting both the organization and its employees.

## Compliance with Labour Laws

Labour laws differ by country, and organizations with remote workers in various locations must ensure compliance with each jurisdiction's labour laws. This includes adhering to local wage and hour laws, tax requirements, overtime regulations, and paid leave policies. Failing to comply with these regulations can lead to legal repercussions and financial penalties.

## Ensuring Data Security and Privacy

With employees accessing sensitive information from various locations, data security becomes a top priority. Organizations must implement cybersecurity protocols, such as multi-factor authentication and secure VPN (Virtual Private Network) access, to protect company data. Additionally, compliance with data protection laws, such as the GDPR (General Data Protection Regulation) for employees in the EU, is essential to prevent data breaches and maintain legal compliance.

## Worker's Compensation and Health and Safety

Employers are responsible for ensuring safe working conditions, even in remote settings. This includes providing ergonomic equipment and ensuring employees have safe home-office setups. Organizations should also be aware of worker's compensation policies and any specific requirements, as remote employees may still be eligible for compensation for work-related injuries that occur at home.

## Employment Contracts and Agreements

Clear employment agreements that outline expectations for remote work are essential. These contracts should address specific terms, such as working hours, availability, data protection, and performance expectations, and may also include clauses for the return of company equipment upon termination. Updating employment contracts to reflect the specific conditions of remote work minimizes misunderstandings and provides a legal foundation for remote arrangements.

Managing remote and hybrid workforces demands a thoughtful approach that addresses both the benefits and complexities these models present. By creating a structured framework for productivity, fostering inclusive communication, and addressing legal considerations, HR can help organizations fully realize the advantages of remote and hybrid work arrangements. As remote work continues to evolve, so too must HR practices, policies, and support systems, ensuring that employees feel connected, valued, and empowered, regardless of where they work.

Organizations that successfully navigate the challenges of remote work position themselves as flexible, adaptive employers of choice, able to attract and retain top talent and remain competitive in a changing world.

## Further Reading

**Fried, Jason, and David Heinemeier.** *Remote: Office Not Required.* Crown Business, 2013.

**Hill, Alison, and Darren Hill.** *Work From Anywhere: The Essential Guide to Becoming a World-Class Hybrid Worker.* Wiley, 2021.

# CHAPTER 13
## EMPLOYEE ENGAGEMENT SURVEYS AND FEEDBACK SYSTEMS

*Employees who believe that management is concerned about them as a whole person – not just an employee – are more productive, more satisfied, more fulfilled. Satisfied employees mean satisfied customers, which leads to profitability.* – **Anne M. Mulcahy**

At Ideal Marketing, employee engagement scores had been slipping, and turnover was on the rise. Concerned, the HR director, Ben, introduced a quarterly engagement survey to gather honest feedback. To encourage transparency, he assured employees that responses were anonymous and that management was committed to making improvements.

One survey highlighted a common issue: employees felt undervalued and disconnected from the company's direction. Many voiced that while the company held regular meetings, their input was rarely sought, and they didn't feel a part of decision-making processes.

Taking this feedback seriously, Ben implemented several changes. He introduced monthly "Listening Sessions," where employees could share ideas with leadership directly. Managers also began holding brief, weekly check-ins focused on career development and team feedback.

Over the next few months, engagement scores improved noticeably. Employees felt heard and valued, and their suggestions led to meaningful changes, like more flexible work hours and clearer communication about company goals. Ben's approach showed that engagement surveys are only powerful when they're backed by genuine action, transforming feedback into a bridge that connects employees and leadership toward a shared vision for the company.

Employee engagement is an essential driver of organizational success. Highly engaged employees are more productive, committed, and satisfied, which directly impacts retention rates, innovation, and overall organizational performance. However, fostering and maintaining employee engagement requires a structured approach to gathering and acting on employee feedback. Engagement surveys and feedback systems are powerful tools that allow HR and leadership to understand employee needs, measure satisfaction, identify challenges, and make data-informed decisions.

This chapter explores the various aspects of developing and utilizing effective engagement surveys and feedback systems. We'll delve into the importance of regular feedback, principles for designing impactful surveys, strategies for interpreting feedback, and how to foster a culture of open communication. By implementing these practices, organizations can build a more engaged, motivated, and high-performing workforce.

## Building an Engaged Workforce

Creating a highly engaged workforce is about cultivating a work environment where employees feel valued, supported, and aligned with organizational goals. Engagement is a result of multiple factors, including strong leadership, meaningful work, growth opportunities, recognition, and a culture of respect.

## Understanding Engagement Drivers

To effectively boost engagement, it's crucial to recognize the key drivers that influence employee satisfaction and motivation. These may include career development opportunities, meaningful job responsibilities, recognition and rewards, supportive management, and a positive work environment. Understanding these elements helps HR design initiatives that support these drivers.

## The Role of Leadership in Engagement

Leaders play a central role in fostering an engaged workforce. Leaders who demonstrate empathy, communicate transparently, and support employee growth tend to inspire greater loyalty and motivation. Leadership training and regular feedback help ensure that managers can effectively support their teams, directly influencing engagement.

## Benefits of an Engaged Workforce

Engaged employees exhibit greater productivity, resilience, and commitment to the organization's vision and goals. This, in turn, enhances the quality of work and strengthens the organization's culture. Furthermore, engaged teams often exhibit lower turnover rates, reducing recruitment costs and preserving institutional knowledge.

# The Importance of Regular Employee Feedback

An employee engagement survey provides valuable insights into the areas where the company is excelling and where it should improve, from an employee's perspective. If done right, these surveys act as a roadmap for creating a more engaging and productive work environment.

Regular feedback channels provide employees with an outlet to voice their opinions, concerns, and suggestions, fostering a culture of inclusivity and trust. Additionally, ongoing feedback helps management identify issues before they escalate and reveals opportunities for improvement.

### Creating a Two-Way Communication Channel

Regular feedback channels promote transparency and show employees that their opinions matter. Organizations should establish a mix of formal and informal feedback mechanisms, including surveys, suggestion boxes, performance reviews, and one-on-one check-ins. Encouraging open communication builds trust and improves employee morale.

## Employee Feedback as an Early Warning System

Employee feedback serves as a valuable early warning system, allowing organizations to address dissatisfaction or disengagement promptly. By regularly gathering insights, organizations can proactively address issues and improve employee satisfaction, reducing the risk of high turnover and productivity dips.

## Linking Feedback to Continuous Improvement

A continuous feedback loop helps organizations adapt to changing employee needs. Regularly asking for feedback shows employees that the organization values improvement and is committed to creating a positive work environment. When feedback is gathered, analyzed, and acted upon consistently, employees feel valued, empowered, and engaged.

# Designing Effective Engagement Surveys

To capture valuable and actionable insights, engagement surveys must be well-designed, focusing on relevance, clarity, and brevity. A thoughtfully crafted survey can accurately measure employee sentiments and identify areas for growth, while a poorly designed one risks employee disengagement and unreliable results.

## Defining Objectives for the Survey

Before creating a survey, define the goals and objectives it aims to achieve. Objectives may include assessing overall job satisfaction, identifying leadership strengths and weaknesses, or understanding employees' career development needs. Clear objectives guide the survey's design and help in focusing on the most pertinent issues.

## Crafting Clear and Relevant Questions

Survey questions should be direct, easily understandable, and tailored to the organization's needs. Using a mix of quantitative (e.g., rating scales) and qualitative (e.g., open-ended questions) methods provides a comprehensive view of employee engagement. Additionally, questions should avoid leading or biased language to ensure honest responses.

## Ensuring Anonymity and Confidentiality

To encourage candid responses, ensure employees that their feedback will remain anonymous and confidential. Employees are more likely to share honest opinions and insights when they know their identities are protected. This anonymity builds trust and contributes to a more accurate portrayal of the workplace climate.

## Timing and Frequency

Deciding on the frequency of engagement surveys is key to balancing valuable insights with potential survey fatigue. Annual or semi-annual surveys provide an overarching view of engagement levels, while quarterly pulse surveys can capture real-time insights and track improvements over time.

**Note:** Appendix 1 contains an example of an Employee Engagement Survey.

# Analyzing Feedback and Taking Action

Once feedback is collected, analyzing it carefully and taking concrete actions based on insights are essential. Effective analysis uncovers patterns and identifies the most pressing issues impacting engagement.

## Data Collection and Analysis Tools

Leveraging data analysis tools, such as HR software with analytics capabilities, can simplify the process of interpreting survey data. HR professionals can categorize responses, track engagement trends over time, and identify recurring themes. Visualizing data with graphs and charts helps in presenting findings to stakeholders clearly and effectively.

## Prioritizing Key Areas for Improvement

After analyzing the data, prioritize the issues that have the most significant impact on engagement. For example, if career development opportunities are a major concern, addressing this area can yield a considerable improvement in overall engagement. Focus on areas that align with organizational goals and are feasible to implement.

## Taking Action and Communicating Results

It's crucial to communicate the survey results to employees, highlighting key findings and planned actions. This transparency shows employees that their feedback was valued and taken seriously. Implementing changes based on feedback builds trust and reinforces a culture of continuous improvement.

## Tracking Progress and Measuring Impact

Once changes are implemented, measure their impact to determine their effectiveness. Follow-up surveys or pulse checks can help track progress and provide additional insights. Organizations should view employee engagement as an evolving process and consistently monitor the effectiveness of their efforts.

## Building a Culture of Open Communication

Beyond formal surveys, fostering a culture of open communication encourages employees to share feedback freely and fosters mutual respect between staff and leadership. Open communication strengthens trust, reduces misunderstandings, and promotes a collaborative work environment.

## Encouraging Openness from Leadership

For open communication to flourish, leaders must model it. Leaders should be transparent in their communication, openly sharing organizational changes, goals, and challenges with employees. Encouraging questions and discussions creates a culture where employees feel comfortable voicing their thoughts and ideas.

## Training Managers to Listen and Respond

Managers play a pivotal role in maintaining open lines of communication with their teams. Training managers to actively listen and respond constructively to employee feedback fosters an environment of respect and understanding. This also enables managers to identify and address issues before they affect engagement.

## Creating Safe Spaces for Feedback

Safe spaces for feedback, such as dedicated feedback sessions, focus groups, or online suggestion boxes, give employees the freedom to share their opinions without fear of judgment. Regularly holding team meetings that encourage open dialogue can strengthen relationships and improve team morale.

## Promoting Transparency in Decision-Making

Transparency in decision-making helps employees feel included in the organization's journey. By sharing the reasoning behind certain decisions, leaders demonstrate respect for employees' intelligence and commitment. Transparent communication contributes to higher morale and deeper trust.

Employee engagement surveys and feedback systems are indispensable tools for understanding and enhancing employee satisfaction and commitment. When thoughtfully designed and implemented, these tools provide valuable insights into the strengths and weaknesses of an organization, allowing HR and leadership to take informed actions. By building an engaged workforce, regularly seeking feedback, designing effective surveys, analyzing responses, and fostering open communication, organizations can create a thriving workplace that attracts and retains top talent.

An engaged workforce is more productive, resilient, and innovative, making engagement strategies a critical component of organizational success. When employees feel heard and valued, they are motivated to contribute their best work and stay committed to the company's mission. As engagement practices evolve, HR's role in supporting these systems remains central to creating a work environment where every employee can flourish.

## Further Reading

**Morgan, Jacob**, *The Employee Experience Advantage: How to Win the War for Talent by Giving Employees the Workspaces they Want, the Tools they Need, and a Culture They Can Celebrate.* Wiley, 2017.

**Pink, Daniel H.** *Drive: The Surprising Truth About What Motivates Us.* Riverhead Books, 2009.

# CHAPTER 14
## CHANGE MANAGEMENT AND ORGANIZATIONAL RESTRUCTURING

*The announcement is the easy part; it makes the manager look bold and decisive. Implementation is more difficult, because no matter how good and compelling the data, there will always be active and passive resistance, rationalizations—particularly when the changes require new ways of working or painful cuts. To get through this, managers have to get their hands dirty, engage their teams to make choices and sometimes confront recalcitrant colleagues.*

**– Ron Ashkenas and Rizwan Khan**

When Central Financial decided to upgrade its outdated software system, the team was apprehensive. The transition meant learning new processes, and for many employees, it felt daunting. Sam, the operations manager, recognized that change was necessary for long-term growth, but he also knew that without the team's buy-in, the transition could fail.

To ease the shift, Sam organized a series of training workshops and created an open forum where employees could ask questions and share concerns. He also designated "change champions" from each department to assist teammates with the new system. By encouraging collaboration and keeping communication open, Sam helped foster a sense of teamwork and trust.

As the weeks passed, the initial resistance began to fade. Employees felt empowered by the support and resources provided, and soon, productivity started improving. Sam's approach to change management showed his team that change, while challenging, could be an opportunity for growth and unity when approached with empathy and a clear plan.

Organizational change and restructuring are inevitable in today's dynamic business environment, and HR plays a crucial role in ensuring these transitions are as smooth and effective as possible. HR's involvement is essential not only in shaping strategies for change but also in supporting employees through each phase of the transition, helping to mitigate anxiety, maintain productivity, and build resilience.

## The Role of HR in Managing Change

In times of change, HR serves as both a strategic partner and a support system for employees. By aligning HR strategies with the organizational goals of the restructuring, HR can drive a successful transformation while addressing employees' concerns.

Key responsibilities for HR in managing change include:

## Identifying and Addressing Concerns Early:

HR should assess potential concerns, resistance, and readiness within the workforce. This helps proactively address challenges and mitigate resistance.

## Implementing Training and Development

Equipping employees with new skills and knowledge needed to succeed in the restructured organization is critical. Training ensures that employees are not only prepared but also empowered to embrace new roles or changes in responsibilities.

## Collaborating with Leadership

Working closely with leadership to ensure clear goals, timelines, and the impact on employees helps align messaging and strategies, enhancing clarity and cohesion throughout the organization.

## Communicating Change Effectively

Effective communication is at the heart of successful change management. The HR department must prioritize transparency, empathy, and clarity to minimize misunderstandings and ease anxieties:

## Developing Clear, Consistent Messaging

Employees need honest, consistent information about the reasons behind the change, what it entails, and how it will impact them. HR should work with leaders to ensure that the messaging reflects the values and future vision of the organization.

## Utilizing Multiple Communication Channels

Given the diversity of communication preferences, a mix of methods such as town hall meetings, one-on-one check-ins, email updates, and video messages helps ensure everyone stays informed.

## Encouraging Feedback and Open Dialogue

Offering opportunities for employees to ask questions and share concerns in a safe, respectful environment can enhance trust. HR should actively listen, address concerns, and adjust communication plans as needed to maintain alignment with employee sentiment.

## Supporting Employees During Organizational Restructuring

During restructuring, HR's role as an employee advocate becomes even more significant. To maintain morale and minimize disruption, HR should prioritize the following:

## Providing Emotional and Career Support

Restructuring often involves role changes, layoffs, or shifts in responsibilities. Offering resources such as counseling services, career workshops, and resume-building sessions can support employees during this challenging time.

## Offering Transitional Support

Employees who face redundancy or role adjustments benefit from outplacement services, such as career coaching and job search assistance, to ease their transition to new opportunities.

## Managing Employee Relations

HR should monitor the organizational climate closely during restructuring to address any emerging conflicts or grievances promptly, ensuring a supportive environment and addressing morale issues.

# Building Resilience During Transition

Building resilience within the organization during times of change is essential for long-term success. HR can foster resilience by cultivating adaptability, encouraging a growth mindset, and reinforcing organizational values.

## Encouraging a Growth Mindset

Training managers to inspire and model resilience helps employees see change as an opportunity for growth. Providing development programs on adaptability and stress management can reinforce this mindset.

## Recognizing and Celebrating Milestones

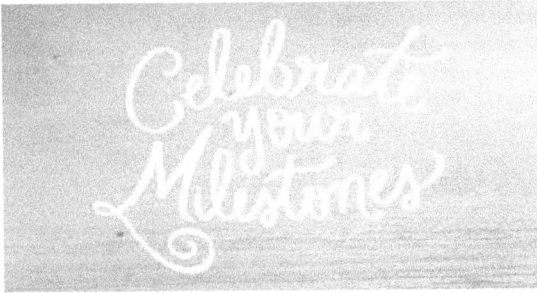

Acknowledging small wins during the change process—such as successful team realignments or the completion of key transition stages—can boost morale and keep employees motivated.

## Reinforcing Organizational Culture and Values

HR can lead initiatives that reaffirm the organization's mission and values, reminding employees of their shared purpose and building a sense of unity that strengthens resilience.

Change management and organizational restructuring are challenging yet crucial processes that shape the future of any organization. For HR professionals, guiding a team through these transitions involves a careful balance of strategic planning, empathetic communication, and unwavering support for employees. By playing an active role in preparing, communicating, and fostering resilience, HR can turn periods of uncertainty into opportunities for growth, unity, and strengthened organizational culture.

As we tackle the complexities of change, it's essential to remember that the human element lies at the heart of successful transitions. When employees feel supported, informed, and valued, they are more likely to embrace change and contribute positively to the organization's evolving goals. With a clear vision and a committed approach, HR can help transform challenges into building blocks for a more adaptable and resilient workforce.

## Further Reading

**Heath, Chip, and Dan Heath.** *Switch: How to Change Things When Change Is Hard.* Crown Business, 2010.

**Kotter, John P.** *Leading Change.* Harvard Business Review Press, 1996.

**Kotter, John P. and Dan S. Cohen.** *The Heart of Change: Real-Life Stories of How People Change Their Organizations.* Harvard Business Review Press, 2002.

# CHAPTER 15
## WORKPLACE SAFETY AND RISK MANAGEMENT

*Ask the people who work in the warehouse to start thinking about safety, and on a regular, periodic basis, review and discuss how they might work better. I encourage people to put a meeting on a calendar, once a month, at least to come together for an hour or 90 minutes to discuss ideas for improvement.*

**— Joseph Flahiff,**

At Evergreen Manufacturing, the production floor was a busy, high-paced environment where safety protocols were essential. One day, James, a new employee eager to prove himself, skipped wearing his protective gloves to complete his tasks faster. During his shift, he sustained a minor injury, sparking concern among his teammates and supervisor.

Anna, the safety manager, took the incident seriously and gathered the team for a quick, open discussion about safety practices. She emphasized that the protocols weren't about slowing anyone down but about protecting everyone on the job. To make it personal, she shared a story of a friend who'd been seriously injured on a job where shortcuts were common.

The conversation resonated with the team, and even James realized the importance of following safety procedures, no matter how small. Anna's commitment to a "safety-first" culture reminded the team that at Evergreen, every protocol was there to ensure they went home safe and sound each day.

Ensuring a safe work environment is a fundamental responsibility for any organization. Workplace safety not only protects employees from harm but also minimizes potential disruptions, legal liabilities, and financial losses. Risk management, as part of a comprehensive safety program, proactively addresses and mitigates hazards, creating a workplace where employees feel secure and focused.

The United States Department of Labor points out that:

*Employers will find that implementing these recommended practices also brings other benefits. Safety and health programs help businesses:*

- *Prevent workplace injuries and illnesses*

- *Improve compliance with laws and regulations*

- *Reduce costs, including significant reductions in workers' compensation premiums*

- *Engage workers*

- ***Enhance*** *their social responsibility goals*

- ***Increase*** *productivity and enhance overall business operations*

Workplace safety is more than adherence to regulatory standards; it is an organizational commitment to protect employees' well-being and foster a culture of vigilance and responsibility. Effective risk management requires identifying potential threats, addressing them proactively, and embedding safety practices into the core of workplace operations. HR plays a central role in promoting safety standards, communicating policies, and supporting efforts to mitigate risks, thus safeguarding both employees and the organization.

# Creating a Safe Work Environment

Establishing a safe work environment is an ongoing effort that requires commitment, consistency, and adaptability:

### Developing Clear Safety Policies and Procedures

Comprehensive policies addressing general workplace safety, emergency response, and accident protocols provide a foundation. These policies should be accessible to all employees and regularly reviewed for relevance.

### Promoting a Safety Culture

HR can encourage a safety-first mindset by providing regular training sessions, recognizing safe practices, and fostering open communication about safety concerns. Building a culture that values safety ensures that all employees actively participate in maintaining a secure workplace.

## Ensuring Compliance with Regulatory Standards

Adhering to national and industry-specific safety regulations, such as OSHA (Occupational Safety and Health Administration) and CCOHS (Canada Center for Occupational Health and Safety) guidelines in the United States and Canada, helps maintain compliance and demonstrates a commitment to employee welfare.

# Identifying and Mitigating Workplace Hazards

An essential aspect of risk management is the continuous identification and mitigation of workplace hazards, which helps prevent accidents and injuries:

## Conducting Regular Safety Audits and Risk Assessments

Routine assessments allow HR and safety teams to identify potential hazards, evaluate existing safety measures, and prioritize areas needing improvement.

## Implementing Preventive Measures

Addressing hazards proactively—such as installing protective equipment, setting up ergonomic workspaces, and enforcing clean-up protocols—minimizes risks. HR should collaborate with facilities management and team leaders to ensure these measures are upheld.

## Training and Awareness Programs

Educating employees on hazard identification, equipment handling, and emergency response procedures enhances their preparedness and ability to respond effectively to potential risks.

## Employee Privacy

Workplace safety measures should balance protecting employees while respecting their privacy:

### Understanding Privacy Rights

HR must respect employees' privacy, particularly with regard to medical and personal information. Safety policies must align with privacy laws, ensuring that any medical information collected for safety purposes remains confidential.

### Balancing Monitoring with Privacy

Privacy concerns must be considered when implementing surveillance or monitoring systems for safety purposes. Transparency with employees about the purpose of these measures and limiting data collection to what is necessary demonstrates respect for personal boundaries.

### Communicating Data Handling Practices

HR should communicate how safety-related data is collected, stored, and used to help employees understand that their privacy rights are respected. This fosters trust and eases concerns over surveillance or data collection measures.

Workplace safety and risk management are essential to an organization's stability and employee welfare. HR professionals can create a safer, more resilient workplace by proactively identifying risks, fostering a culture of safety, and balancing the need for security with respect for privacy. The ultimate goal is to protect employees while enabling them to perform their roles without fear of preventable harm, fostering a work environment that values security and responsibility.

Through consistent effort, transparency, and employee engagement, HR can drive initiatives that not only meet regulatory standards but exceed them, contributing to a work environment that prioritizes safety as a core organizational value.

## Further Reading

**Goetsch, David L.** *The Safety Professional's Handbook: Technical Applications.* American Society of Safety Engineers (ASSE), 2019.

**Jain, Aditya, Suvi Nenonen, and David Walters.** *Managing Health, Safety, and Well-Being: Ethics, Responsibility, and Sustainability.* Springer International Publishing, 2021.

# CHAPTER 16
## EMPLOYEE DISCIPLINE AND TERMINATION PROCESSES

*Euphemism in the workplace does not end with job descriptions. It reaches a pusillanimous peak at the other end of the work process - in dismissal.*

**- Nigel Rees**

When Sophie, a manager at Applewood Tech, noticed repeated issues with Sam's performance and missed deadlines, she decided to address it with a series of corrective discussions. Though Sam was a talented developer, his lack of commitment was affecting team morale. Sophie tried to provide support, offering resources for time management and clear guidance on expectations. Despite these efforts, Sam's performance didn't improve.

After months of coaching, Sophie made the difficult decision to initiate a formal termination process. During their meeting, she approached the conversation with empathy, acknowledging Sam's skills and encouraging him to find a role better suited to his strengths. She ensured that he understood the reasons for the decision and gave him ample time to ask questions.

Though the situation was tough, Sophie's respectful approach helped Sam leave with his dignity intact. She reminded the team that discipline wasn't about punishment but about accountability and fairness to everyone. The experience reinforced the company's commitment to handling terminations with respect, showing that even in difficult moments, integrity and compassion come first.

Employee discipline and termination are delicate but essential aspects of managing a workforce. When handled thoughtfully and consistently, these processes not only uphold organizational standards but also help maintain morale and productivity within the team. Effective discipline and fair termination procedures protect the rights of both employees and employers, balancing organizational needs with the well-being and dignity of employees. This chapter covers essential steps for handling disciplinary issues, conducting fair investigations, and managing the termination process respectfully while mitigating legal risks.

## Handling Disciplinary Issues Fairly

Discipline should be approached as an opportunity to correct behaviour and enhance performance. Key principles include transparency, consistency, and constructive feedback.

## Establishing Clear Policies

Before implementing disciplinary action, organizations should establish clear policies and guidelines on acceptable behaviour, performance expectations, and consequences for infractions. Employees should be made aware of these policies during onboarding and regularly reminded through communication channels, reinforcing clarity around standards and expectations.

A sample Disciplinary Action Policy is contained in Appendix 2.

## Implementing Progressive Discipline

Progressive discipline, where penalties escalate with repeat infractions, offers employees opportunities to improve before facing severe consequences. A typical approach might begin with a verbal warning, followed by a written warning, suspension, and, if necessary, termination. This method ensures a fair chance for employees to address their shortcomings while protecting the organization.

## Maintaining Objectivity and Fairness

Supervisors should treat all employees equally in the disciplinary process, avoiding favouritism or personal biases. Documenting disciplinary actions ensures accountability and provides a record if issues escalate or legal questions arise.

# Conducting Investigations and Documentation

Investigating disciplinary issues thoroughly and documenting them accurately is critical for an effective resolution process.

## Conducting Fact-Based Investigations

Investigations should be objective and fact-based, seeking input from relevant parties and witnesses while respecting confidentiality. Ensuring that all involved have an opportunity to share their perspective is crucial for understanding the situation accurately.

## Accurate and Detailed Documentation

Documentation should include the details of the incident, the employee's response, and the outcome of the investigation. This may include written warnings, performance improvement plans, and any other relevant communications. Keeping records ensures that decisions are based on evidence, which can be invaluable in case of disputes or legal scrutiny.

# Managing Terminations with Dignity and Respect

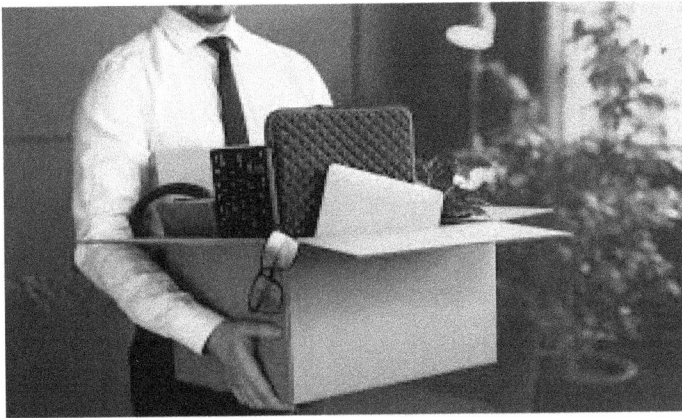

Terminations, though sometimes necessary, are often the most challenging responsibility for managers. Managing the process with compassion and professionalism can make a significant difference.

## Conducting the Termination Meeting

Termination meetings should be conducted in private and with a witness, typically a representative from HR, to ensure documentation and support. The conversation should be direct and clear, focusing on the decision rather than engaging in extensive justification or debate.

## Providing Support and Resources

Offering transitional support, such as career counseling or severance packages, can ease the impact on the employee. While optional, these gestures help protect the organization's reputation and leave the employee with a more positive view of the company.

# Navigating Legal Risks in Employee Dismissal

Understanding and mitigating the legal risks surrounding termination protects the organization and ensures fair treatment.

## Ensuring Legal Compliance

Employers must comply with labour laws and anti-discrimination statutes to avoid wrongful termination claims. This includes respecting employee rights regarding notice periods, severance payments, and other statutory requirements.

## Guarding Against Retaliation Claims

Employers should be cautious when terminating employees who have recently filed complaints or raised concerns, as this may appear retaliatory. Maintaining clear documentation of performance issues and previous warnings is crucial in demonstrating that the termination is unrelated to such actions.

Employee discipline and termination require a careful approach that balances organizational needs with individual dignity and fairness. By following fair procedures, documenting issues meticulously, and managing terminations with compassion, organizations can ensure a respectful and legally sound process.

## Further Reading

**Butler, T.** *The HR Guide to Managing Workplace Investigations.* SHRM Press, 2021.

**Kelly, H.** *Managing Employee Discipline: A Practical Guide.* Routledge, 2019.

# CHAPTER 17
## ENHANCING
## EMPLOYEE RELATIONS

*Employees who believe that management is concerned about them as a whole person – not just an employee – are more productive, more satisfied, more fulfilled. Satisfied employees mean satisfied customers, which leads to profitability.* – **Anne Mulcahy**

At Wilson Manufacturing, tensions between management and employees had been simmering for months, resulting in high turnover and widespread dissatisfaction. The CEO, Lisa Carter, recognized that employee relations needed urgent attention. She initiated an open-door policy, encouraging honest conversations between managers and employees about challenges they faced in their roles. This open dialogue allowed employees to voice concerns, and managers to offer more meaningful support.

Lisa also introduced regular town hall meetings where employees could raise issues directly, fostering transparency. Additionally, team-building workshops helped improve camaraderie between departments, breaking down communication barriers.

Collaboration with the union played a critical role in rebuilding trust. By working more cooperatively, management was able to address grievances fairly and efficiently. Within a year, employee satisfaction had noticeably improved, turnover had decreased, and productivity surged. The culture at Wilson Manufacturing was transformed from one of tension to one of trust and collaboration, driven by Lisa's commitment to open communication and strong employee relations.

Employee relations are at the heart of a successful organization. Positive, productive relationships between employees and management foster a workplace culture where trust, collaboration, and motivation thrive. In an environment where employee relations are nurtured, team members feel respected, valued, and empowered to contribute their best work. This chapter explores the key aspects of building strong relationships between managers and employees, improving communication channels, addressing the role of HR and unions, and promoting trust, transparency, and collaboration within the workplace.

## Building Strong Relationships Between Managers and Employees

The relationship between managers and their team members sets the tone for overall employee engagement and satisfaction. A strong, positive manager-employee relationship helps enhance performance, reduces turnover, and promotes job satisfaction.

## Empathy and Understanding

Empathy is one of the most important qualities in fostering positive relationships. When managers take the time to understand their employees' concerns, challenges, and aspirations, it creates a supportive environment where employees feel heard and valued. Managers who lead with empathy can more effectively address employee needs, boost morale, and foster loyalty.

## Regular One-on-One Meetings

Scheduling regular one-on-one meetings allows managers to provide individualized support, feedback, and guidance. These sessions also offer employees a chance to voice concerns, seek clarification, or express career ambitions. When managers consistently engage with their team on a personal level, trust builds naturally.

## Recognition and Feedback

Positive recognition is a key motivator for employees. Regularly recognizing achievements—whether through verbal praise, rewards, or public acknowledgment—boosts morale and reinforces the desired behaviours. Constructive feedback should also be provided, but in a way that encourages growth without discouraging the employee.

# Improving Communication Channels

Effective communication is essential for healthy employee relations. Poor communication leads to misunderstandings, confusion, and frustration, while clear, open communication strengthens workplace relationships and promotes efficiency.

## Open-Door Policies

An open-door policy encourages employees to communicate freely with their managers without fear of reprisal or judgment. It creates a transparent environment where employees can raise concerns, ask questions, or offer suggestions at any time. By fostering a culture of openness, employees feel empowered and valued, contributing to a more positive work atmosphere.

## Use of Multiple Communication Channels

In today's diverse workplace, employees prefer a variety of communication methods—emails, face-to-face meetings, video calls, instant messaging, and team collaboration tools. Offering multiple communication options accommodates different preferences and ensures that critical information is accessible to all.

## Encouraging Upward Communication

Upward communication—where feedback and ideas come from employees to management—is just as important as downward communication. Encouraging upward communication enables management to identify problems early and gain insights into how workplace processes can be improved from those on the front lines. Organizations that incorporate upward communication effectively are generally better able to serve the needs of their employees, **increasing engagement and satisfaction levels.**

## HR and Unions

Human Resources (HR) and unions play a crucial role in employee relations by acting as mediators between the organization and its workforce. HR departments focus on managing employee benefits, handling conflicts, and promoting professional development, while unions represent employees' rights and ensure that their voices are heard on matters such as wages, working conditions, and job security.

## HR as a Facilitator of Positive Relations

HR departments are pivotal in maintaining good employee relations by creating policies that protect employee rights, fostering workplace fairness, and implementing programs that support employee well-being. HR also plays a key role in onboarding new hires, addressing employee grievances, and facilitating conflict resolution.

## Role of Unions

In workplaces with union representation, unions play a central role in employee relations by advocating for workers' rights, negotiating collective bargaining agreements, and ensuring fair treatment. A healthy relationship between management and unions leads to mutually beneficial outcomes, as both sides work together to resolve disputes and create a more productive work environment.

# The Role of Trust and Transparency in the Workplace

Trust and transparency are fundamental to a healthy organizational culture. Employees who trust their leaders are more likely to feel engaged, motivated, and committed to the company's goals. Conversely, a lack of transparency can breed distrust, disengagement, and even conflict.

## Building Trust Through Open Communication

Transparency in communication—whether it's about company performance, future plans, or changes in the workplace—is critical to building trust. Employees want to be kept in the loop and understand how decisions will affect them. When leaders are honest and forthcoming, it fosters a culture of openness, leading to greater trust and collaboration.

## Trusting Employees with Responsibility

Empowering employees with responsibility and decision-making authority demonstrates trust in their abilities. When employees feel trusted, they are more likely to take ownership of their work and approach tasks with a sense of accountability.

## Admitting Mistakes

Leaders who admit mistakes and take responsibility create a culture of accountability and trust. Transparency about errors shows employees that it's okay to make mistakes, as long as there is a focus on learning and improving.

## Fostering Collaboration and Team Spirit

A collaborative work environment helps employees feel connected, valued, and more aligned with the organization's goals. Teamwork also fosters creativity and innovation as employees pool their skills and perspectives.

## Cross-Departmental Collaboration

Encouraging collaboration across different departments or teams allows employees to broaden their perspectives, develop new skills, and improve problem-solving capabilities. Cross-functional teams also promote a sense of community within the workplace.

## Team Building Activities

Team-building exercises—whether formal or informal—are great tools for fostering collaboration and team spirit. From workshops to retreats or even social gatherings, these activities help build relationships, reduce barriers, and promote a sense of belonging.

## Encouraging a Culture of Shared Goals

A collaborative workplace thrives on shared goals and mutual respect. Encouraging employees to work towards common objectives—rather than individual success—fosters a team-oriented mindset. Leaders should clearly communicate how each team member's contribution helps achieve larger organizational goals, reinforcing the idea that collaboration is key to success.

## Further Reading

**Aylott, Elizabeth.** *Employee Relations: Putting the Employee at the Heart of Your Business.* Kogan Page, 2018.

**Daniels, Kathy.** *Employee Relations in an Organizational Context.* CIPD, 2020.

**Gennard, John, and Graham Judge.** *Managing Employment Relations.* Chartered Institute of Personnel and Development (CIPD), 2016.

# CHAPTER 18
## HR TECHNOLOGY
## AND AUTOMATION

*I think what makes AI different from other technologies is that it's going to bring humans and machines closer together. AI is sometimes incorrectly framed as machines replacing humans. It's not about machines replacing humans, but machines augmenting humans. Humans and machines have different relative strengths and weaknesses, and it's about the combination of these two that will allow human intents and business process to scale 10x, 100x, and beyond that in the coming years. –* **Robin Bordoli,**

The HR team at Little Giant was overwhelmed by manual processes—especially onboarding new hires, which involved hours of paperwork and endless emails. Realizing the need for change, David, the HR director, decided to implement an HR software system to automate repetitive tasks like payroll, time-off requests, and employee onboarding.

The team was initially skeptical, worried the software might feel impersonal or overly complicated. But David arranged training sessions to demonstrate how it could simplify their workload and free up time for more meaningful interactions with employees. Within a few weeks, the team saw the benefits firsthand—new hires could complete forms online before their start date, payroll was processed more accurately, and employees could view their benefits information with a click.

With technology handling the mundane tasks, David and his team had more time to focus on career development and building stronger connections with employees. Embracing automation taught the team that, rather than replacing human touch, technology could empower them to be even more attentive and proactive in their roles.

Technology has transformed the HR landscape, revolutionizing how organizations attract, engage, and manage talent. From streamlining recruitment and onboarding to leveraging data for strategic decisions, technology has become a vital component of effective HR operations. This chapter explores key technologies and automation trends that enable HR teams to operate more efficiently, make data-driven decisions, and enhance the employee experience.

## The Rise of Tech: Tools for Recruitment, Onboarding, and Performance Management

HR technology spans multiple facets, including tools for recruitment, onboarding, and performance management.

## Recruitment Tools

Applicant Tracking Systems (ATS) simplify the recruitment process by helping HR teams post jobs, track applications, and screen candidates efficiently. Platforms like LinkedIn Recruiter, Greenhouse, and Workable use AI to analyze resumes and recommend candidates, speeding up hiring without compromising on quality.

## Onboarding Software

Onboarding tools like BambooHR, Workday, and Gusto streamline the onboarding experience, enabling new hires to complete documentation, review company policies, and connect with team members. Automating this process helps new employees feel welcome and engaged, ultimately improving retention.

## Performance Management Systems

In Chapter 4, we discussed Performance Management. Platforms such as Lattice, SAP SuccessFactors, and 15Five facilitate regular feedback, goal-setting, and performance reviews. These systems encourage consistent communication, allowing managers and employees to set realistic objectives, track progress, and identify areas for improvement.

## Automating HR Processes for Efficiency

Automation enhances HR efficiency by minimizing repetitive tasks and freeing up time for strategic initiatives.

## Payroll and Benefits Administration

Payroll and benefits systems like ADP, Paylocity, and Zenefits automate the calculation and distribution of salaries, deductions, and benefits, ensuring accuracy and compliance. Automating these processes not only saves time but also reduces errors and enhances employee satisfaction.

## Leave Management

Leave management tools simplify tracking and approving paid time off, sick leave, and other absences. Platforms like Deputy and Kronos help managers and HR departments stay informed about availability while giving employees easy access to leave balances.

## Employee Self-Service

Employee self-service portals provide employees with access to essential information, such as pay stubs, tax documents, and personal information updates. This functionality empowers employees and reduces the administrative burden on HR.

## Using Data Analytics to Drive HR Decisions

Data analytics in HR is transforming how organizations approach talent management and decision-making.

## Employee Performance Analytics

Performance data allows HR to identify high achievers, spot trends in employee development, and address underperformance effectively. By analyzing metrics like productivity, engagement scores, and training completion rates, HR can offer targeted interventions to improve individual and team performance.

## Turnover and Retention Analysis

Predictive analytics tools can analyze patterns in turnover and help HR identify factors that contribute to employee departures. These data can inform retention strategies, such as targeted benefits, flexible work options, or enhanced career development programs.

## Diversity and Inclusion Metrics

Using data to monitor diversity metrics allows HR to assess progress on diversity and inclusion initiatives, ensuring a fair and equitable workplace. Tracking metrics related to gender, ethnicity, and age representation enables organizations to build a diverse and inclusive culture.

# The Future of AI in HR

Artificial Intelligence (AI) is reshaping HR by enhancing efficiency and improving decision-making.

## AI-Powered Recruitment and Screening

AI-driven recruitment tools, such as chatbots and automated candidate screening, save HR teams time by assessing resumes and matching candidates with job descriptions. These tools minimize bias and improve the accuracy of candidate selection, allowing HR to focus on strategic aspects of hiring.

## Sentiment Analysis for Employee Engagement

AI can analyze employee feedback, emails, and surveys to gauge sentiment and assess engagement levels. These data can alert HR to potential morale issues and support timely interventions to improve workplace satisfaction.

# Personalized Learning and Development

AI-based learning platforms, such as LinkedIn Learning and Coursera, can analyze employee skills and recommend tailored learning pathways, helping organizations build specific competencies within their workforce.

HR technology and automation have become essential in optimizing HR functions and fostering a more productive and engaged workforce. By automating processes, leveraging data insights, and preparing for AI advancements, organizations can make HR a more efficient, data-driven function. Embracing technology in HR is not only about efficiency but also about enhancing the overall employee experience, building a culture of inclusivity, and making strategic contributions to organizational success.

## Further Reading

**Meister, Jeanne, and Kevin Mulcahy.** *The Future Workplace Experience: 10 Rules for Mastering Disruption in Recruiting and Engaging Employees.* McGraw-Hill Education, 2016.

**Ulrich, Dave, Justin Allen, Wayne Brockbank, Jon Younger, and Mark Nyman.** *HR Transformation: Building Human Resources from the Outside In.* McGraw-Hill Education, 2012.

# CHAPTER 19
## CRISIS MANAGEMENT: HR'S ROLE IN HANDLING EMERGENCIES

*In crisis management, be quick with the facts and slow with the blame.* — **Leonard Saffir.**

BrightWave Tech, a cloud services company, experienced a cybersecurity breach that compromised sensitive client data. On discovering the breach, HR collaborated with IT and communications to contain the impact and support employees.

HR and IT informed employees promptly, shared steps for security, and set up a dedicated channel for updates and questions. HR facilitated remote work for non-essential staff to reduce network activity while IT worked to secure data access for critical roles.

HR activated mental health resources through the Employee Assistance Program and held Q&A sessions to ease concerns over personal data and job security. HR also assisted communications in crafting transparent messages to clients, establishing a hotline for inquiries and helping the client service team handle calls sensitively. After resolving the breach, HR coordinated a review, updated policies, conducted mandatory cybersecurity training, and gathered feedback to improve future responses.

ScienceDirect defines crisis management as follows:

*Crisis management refers to the process of handling a major event that poses a threat to or has already harmed an organization, with the aim of protecting human life, resources, and the organization's reputation. It involves activities such as rescue operations, coordination with emergency services, issuing press reports, and maintaining effective communication.*

https://www.sciencedirect.com/topics/nursing-and-health-professions/crisis-management

In times of crisis, HR plays a critical role in maintaining organizational stability and supporting employees. Whether facing natural disasters, pandemics, or other emergencies, HR must respond with strategies that prioritize safety, ensure business continuity, and address employee needs. By establishing preparedness plans, HR can mitigate disruptions and foster resilience within the workforce. This chapter examines key elements of crisis management, from planning and continuity to employee support and lessons learned.

# Preparing for Natural Disasters, Pandemics, and Other Crises

Crisis preparedness begins with identifying potential risks and developing comprehensive plans.

## Natural Disasters

Natural disasters like hurricanes, earthquakes, and floods can disrupt business operations and endanger employees. HR should work with safety and facility teams to develop evacuation plans, conduct regular drills, and communicate procedures to all employees.

## Pandemics and Health Emergencies

The COVID-19 pandemic highlighted the need for health-related crisis management. HR should establish protocols for remote work, workplace sanitation, and sick leave policies. Maintaining communication channels ensures employees are informed about changes to health guidelines and work policies.

## Cybersecurity Breaches

Cyber threats are an increasingly prevalent risk that can compromise data and disrupt operations. HR plays a role by ensuring that employees understand cybersecurity best practices and are prepared to respond to breaches through secure communication channels.

## HR's Role in Business Continuity Planning

Business continuity planning (BCP) ensures that critical operations can continue during and after a crisis. The following steps are essential:

## Identifying Critical Roles and Resources

HR should identify essential personnel and functions that must operate regardless of disruptions. Creating a succession plan for critical roles ensures that leadership and decision-making capabilities remain intact.

## Developing Contingency Plans

Contingency plans are vital for maintaining productivity in the face of power outages, communication failures, or transportation disruptions. HR should work with IT and operations to establish remote work setups, alternative communication platforms, and resources to support flexible work arrangements.

## Training and Simulations

Regular crisis simulations and training sessions help prepare employees for potential scenarios. Training not only increases individual preparedness but also promotes a culture of readiness and resilience across the organization.

## Supporting Employees During Crises

HR's support is invaluable to employees dealing with difficult circumstances, ensuring both logistical and emotional support.

## Communicating with Transparency and Frequency

Clear, timely, and accurate communication from HR is essential in maintaining confidence and reducing panic. HR should establish reliable channels, such as email updates, company portals, and text alerts, to keep employees informed of the organization's status and response plans.

## Providing Access to Resources

During crises, employees may need access to additional resources, including mental health support, financial assistance, or housing options. HR can provide support by connecting employees with counseling services, Employee Assistance Programs (EAPs), and community aid.

## Flexible Policies for Crisis Adaptation

Allowing flexible work policies, such as adjusted hours or remote work options, demonstrates empathy and support for employees facing personal challenges during a crisis. HR can also assist by implementing temporary leave policies or adjusting deadlines to help employees balance work with personal needs.

## Lessons Learned from Crisis Management

Reflecting on crisis management experiences enables HR to enhance future preparedness and response.

## Analyzing Response Effectiveness

After a crisis, HR should review the effectiveness of its response, assessing areas where the organization excelled and where improvements are needed. Collecting feedback from employees, managers, and crisis response teams provides valuable insights for refining future strategies.

## Updating Policies and Procedures

Crises often reveal gaps in policies and procedures. HR should take the opportunity to update existing policies on remote work, emergency leave, communication, and employee health. Documenting the crisis response in detail serves as a foundation for developing or revising a crisis manual.

## Strengthening Collaboration

Effective crisis management relies on collaboration among HR, leadership, and external partners. Lessons from past crises can help strengthen partnerships with local emergency services, government agencies, and other organizations.

## Ensuring Employee Wellbeing Post-Crisis

Supporting employees' well-being after a crisis is essential for recovery and long-term resilience.

## Offering Mental Health Support

Crises can have lasting psychological effects, leading to anxiety, stress, and burnout. HR should promote mental health resources, such as counseling services, stress management workshops, and wellness programs. Encouraging open conversations about mental health fosters a supportive workplace culture.

## Recognizing Employee Contributions

Acknowledging employees' efforts during crises shows appreciation and builds morale. HR can organize recognition programs, small rewards, or events to celebrate resilience and express gratitude, thereby strengthening team bonds.

## Monitoring Wellbeing Over Time

Crisis recovery is a gradual process, and employee well-being should be monitored continuously. HR can conduct pulse surveys, hold one-on-one check-ins, and solicit feedback to assess how employees are coping and adjust support initiatives as needed.

## Further Reading

**Norris, Wayne.** *Emergency Management for Business: 10 Steps to Protect Your Business and Minimize Losses.* McGraw-Hill Education, 2020.

**Watters, Jamie.** *Disaster Recovery, Crisis Response, and Business Continuity: A Management Desk Reference.* IBM Press, 2014.

# CHAPTER 20
## THE FUTURE OF
## HUMAN RESOURCES

*You have employees working from mobile phones, laptops, from home and even at staycations, which makes the future of work very pleasant.* – **Krunal Patel**

At BrightTech Innovations, HR leader Mia had long been passionate about helping her company stay on the cutting edge of employee engagement and workplace culture. When the team introduced a flexible work-from-anywhere policy, Mia realized she was shaping a new model for employee satisfaction and productivity. She implemented digital tools for collaboration and weekly "virtual watercooler" chats to maintain team cohesion. As BrightTech flourished, Mia's efforts became an inspiration, showing how HR could lead meaningful, forward-thinking change and contribute to long-term success. Her work exemplified HR's evolving role, proving it could be a powerful driver of innovation in the modern workplace.

# Emerging Trends in HR Management

The future of HR management is marked by rapid technological advancements and evolving workforce expectations. Key trends include:

## AI and Automation

Increasingly, HR is using artificial intelligence (AI) to streamline hiring, onboarding, and performance management, freeing HR professionals to focus on more strategic tasks. Predictive analytics are now used to foresee retention risks and automated chatbots handle employee queries, creating a more efficient HR workflow.

## Employee Experience as a Priority

As competition for talent intensifies, companies are placing a strong focus on creating a positive employee experience. From personalized career paths to mental health resources, HR's role is expanding to enhance every aspect of an employee's journey within the organization.

## Skills-Based Hiring

With traditional roles evolving, HR departments are shifting to skills-based hiring and training to help employees adapt to changing job demands. Upskilling and reskilling programs are growing in importance, ensuring the workforce remains agile and competitive.

# The Role of HR in Shaping the Future Workplace

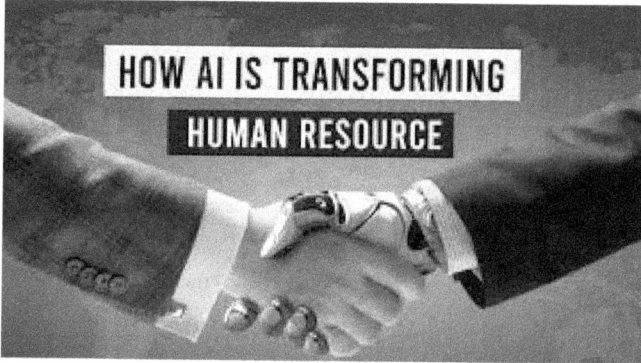

HR is increasingly influential in defining what the future workplace will look like. From crafting policies that support remote and hybrid work models to building inclusive, diverse, and sustainable company cultures, HR leaders play a critical role in designing workplaces that reflect modern values. They are instrumental in making the workplace more flexible, supporting employees' mental health, and driving corporate social responsibility initiatives that attract and retain top talent.

With a focus on creating environments where employees feel valued, HR departments can help their companies not only adapt to change but thrive in it. Their input is essential in aligning workforce needs with company goals, and they act as the bridge between employee expectations and organizational strategy.

# Addressing the Challenges of a Multigenerational Workplace

Today's workforce includes employees from multiple generations, each with different perspectives, communication styles, and expectations. Managing this diversity requires HR to:

## Promote Flexibility in Policies

Flexible work schedules, learning opportunities, and tailored benefits cater to the diverse needs of various age groups, helping create a more inclusive and appealing work environment.

## Encourage Cross-Generational Mentorship

By pairing employees from different generations, HR can foster an exchange of skills and perspectives, strengthening collaboration and mutual respect within the workplace.

## Provide Ongoing Education on Unconscious Bias and Inclusivity

This ensures that all generations are treated equitably, promoting understanding and reducing potential conflicts stemming from generational differences.

# The Evolution of HR's Role in Business Strategy

The traditional view of HR as primarily a transactional department is shifting. HR leaders now occupy strategic positions within organizations, contributing to decisions that directly impact business growth and sustainability. By using data analytics, HR departments can identify trends in employee engagement, performance, and retention, which inform critical business decisions.

HR professionals are also increasingly involved in corporate planning and risk management, with their insights influencing everything from organizational restructuring to succession planning. The move toward strategic partnership means that HR is not only supporting company goals but actively shaping them, contributing to sustainable growth and competitive advantage.

## Further Reading

**Ulrich, Dave, Jon Younger, Wayne Brockbank, and Mike Ulrich**, *HR from the Outside In: Six Competencies for the Future of Human Resources.* McGraw-Hill Education, 2012.

**Meister, Jeanne C., and Kevin J. Mulcahy**, *The Future Workplace Experience: 10 Rules for Mastering Disruption in Recruiting and Engaging Employees.* McGraw-Hill Education, 2016.

# CONCLUSION

## Facing the Future of Human Resources

As we conclude *Mastering HR Challenges: A Comprehensive Guide for HR Professionals*, it's essential to reflect on the evolving landscape of human resources and the critical role HR professionals play in shaping modern organizations. The challenges discussed throughout this book—from talent acquisition and retention to diversity, technology, and employee well-being—highlight the dynamic and multifaceted nature of HR in today's world. This conclusion aims to summarize key insights, reinforce the strategic importance of HR, and look ahead to future opportunities for growth and impact.

## The Evolving Role of HR in Modern Organizations

In recent years, the HR function has expanded far beyond its traditional scope of recruitment and compliance. HR professionals are now strategic partners, working alongside other organizational leaders to cultivate a culture that aligns with business objectives, drives innovation, and fosters inclusivity.

As discussed throughout this book, HR plays a critical role in:

**Driving Organizational Culture:** HR professionals are the architects of workplace culture, responsible for building environments where employees feel valued, motivated, and empowered to achieve their best work.

**Promoting Diversity and Inclusion:** Diversity, equity, and inclusion (DEI) are now core pillars of organizational success. By prioritizing these values, HR can build more cohesive, innovative, and resilient teams.

**Navigating Digital Transformation:** The advent of AI, data analytics, and digital platforms has reshaped the HR function. Embracing these technologies enables HR to streamline processes, make data-driven decisions, and enhance the employee experience.

**Supporting Employee Health and Wellness:** Acknowledging and addressing the holistic needs of employees is essential in a competitive talent market. By fostering wellness, HR not only promotes productivity but also supports the long-term sustainability of the workforce.

Through these functions, HR is positioned as a key driver of organizational resilience and adaptability in the face of rapid change.

## Key Takeaways for Addressing HR Challenges

This book has explored numerous strategies and approaches for managing common HR challenges.

Below are some of the critical takeaways that HR professionals should carry forward:

## Adaptability and Lifelong Learning

HR is a field in constant flux, requiring professionals to stay abreast of changes in labour laws, market trends, and technological advancements. Continuous learning and adaptability are crucial for staying relevant and effective.

## People-Centric Strategy

While technology is transforming HR, a people-first approach remains central to its success. Understanding employee needs, motivations, and concerns allows HR to develop policies that not only enhance productivity but also promote job satisfaction and loyalty.

## Data-Driven Decision Making

The use of analytics in HR enables professionals to forecast trends, assess workforce needs, and make informed strategic decisions. Embracing data allows HR to quantify its impact and contribute to organizational goals more effectively.

## Emphasis on DEI Initiatives

Prioritizing diversity, equity, and inclusion is not just a social obligation but also a business imperative. Organizations that embrace DEI foster creativity, improve employee engagement, and enhance their reputation, making DEI a critical aspect of HR strategy.

## Employee Wellness and Work-Life Balance

Addressing physical, mental, and emotional well-being is essential for talent retention. Employee wellness programs, flexible work options, and supportive policies can help HR create a positive, sustainable work environment.

## The Future of HR: Opportunities and Challenges

Looking forward, HR faces an exciting but challenging future. Rapid technological changes, shifting workforce demographics, and evolving employee expectations will shape the HR profession in unprecedented ways. Here are some trends and opportunities that HR professionals should anticipate:

- **Rise of Artificial Intelligence in HR:** AI is expected to further revolutionize recruitment, performance management, and employee engagement. HR professionals must be prepared to harness AI effectively while addressing ethical concerns related to data privacy and bias.

- **Greater Emphasis on Remote and Hybrid Work Models:** As remote and hybrid work become the norm, HR will need to adapt policies, redefine performance metrics, and create inclusive virtual environments that foster connectivity and collaboration.

- **Focus on Reskilling and Upskilling:** As automation changes the skills landscape, HR will play a vital role in upskilling existing employees and attracting talent with emerging skills. Investment in learning and development will be crucial for future-ready organizations.

- **Prioritizing Sustainability and Corporate Social Responsibility (CSR):** Today's employees seek purpose-driven organizations. HR will increasingly contribute to CSR initiatives, integrating environmental and social considerations into the workplace culture.

The future will also demand HR professionals to be versatile, agile, and visionary leaders capable of managing both challenges and opportunities with a long-term perspective.

## Final Reflections

*Mastering HR Challenges: A Comprehensive Guide for HR Professionals* has provided insights, tools, and strategies to navigate the complexities of modern HR. From fostering inclusivity and managing technological shifts to prioritizing employee wellness and building adaptive cultures, HR professionals are uniquely positioned to make a transformative impact on their organizations.

The work of HR is not only about managing people but also about inspiring and empowering them. By recognizing the potential in each employee, HR professionals have the power to shape futures, build stronger teams, and drive organizational success. The journey may be challenging, but the rewards—fulfilled employees, thriving businesses, and resilient workplace communities—are well worth the effort.

As HR continues to evolve, may this guide serve as a valuable resource, inspiring HR professionals to lead with compassion, innovation, and unwavering commitment to creating workplaces that uplift individuals and achieve collective success.

# APPENDIX 1

## Sample Employee Engagement Survey

### Instructions:

Your feedback is important in helping us understand your experience and improve our work environment. Please rate each statement on a scale of **1-5**, where:

- **1 = Strongly Disagree**
- **2 = Disagree**
- **3 = Neutral**
- **4 = Agree**
- **5 = Strongly Agree**

Your responses are confidential and will only be used to enhance our workplace.

### Section 1: Leadership and Vision

I understand the company's vision and
how my role contributes to it.          1   2   3   4   5

Leadership provides a clear direction
for our team.                           1   2   3   4   5

My manager effectively communicates our
team goals.                             1   2   3   4   5

I feel supported by leadership in achieving
my professional goals.          1  2  3  4  5

I have confidence in the leadership's decisions
regarding the future of
the company.          1  2  3  4  5

## Section 2: Empowerment and Autonomy

I have the resources and tools I need to do my
job effectively.          1  2  3  4  5

I feel encouraged to make decisions that
impact my work.          1  2  3  4  5

I have opportunities to take initiative
in my role.          1  2  3  4  5

I feel trusted by my manager to handle my
responsibilities without excessive
oversight.          1  2  3  4  5

My feedback and ideas are valued by my
team and manager.          1  2  3  5  5

## Section 3: Professional Development and Growth

I have opportunities to learn new skills in
my current role.          1  2  3  4  5

My manager encourages my professional
development.          1  2  3  4  5

I am satisfied with the career growth
opportunities available to me here.  1  2  3  4  5

I receive regular feedback that helps me
improve my performance.          1   2   3   4   5

I feel supported in setting and achieving my
career goals.                    1   2   3   4   5

## Section 4: Recognition and Rewards

My contributions are recognized and appreciated by
my manager.                      1   2   3   4   5

I feel valued for the work I do.    1   2   3   4   5

The reward system here is fair
and motivating.                  1   2   3   4   5

I am satisfied with the benefits and perks provided
by the company.                  1   2   3   4   5

I receive recognition from my peers for my
accomplishments.                 1   2   3   4   5

## Section 5: Communication and Feedback

Communication within my team is effective
and clear.                       1   2   3   4   5

I feel comfortable voicing my ideas and
concerns to my manager.          1   2   3   4   5

Feedback from my manager is constructive
and timely.                      1   2   3   4   5

I am kept informed about important company
decisions that affect my work.   1   2   3   4   5

My manager is accessible when I need guidance
or support.                     1   2   3   4   5

# Section 6: Work Environment and Culture

I feel like a valued member of
my team.                          1   2   3   4   5

There is a strong sense of collaboration within
my team.                          1   2   3   4   5

Our work environment encourages respect
and inclusivity.               1   2   3   4   5

I am satisfied with the work-life balance
provided by the company.       1   2   3   4   5

I believe the company genuinely cares about
employee well-being.           1   2   3   4   5

# Section 7: Overall Satisfaction and Engagement

I am proud to work for this
company.                          1   2   3   4   5

I would recommend this company as a great
place to work.                1   2   3   4   5

I am motivated to contribute to the company's
success.                         1   2   3   4   5

I see myself working here for the foreseeable
future.                          1   2   3   4   5

I feel engaged and enthusiastic
about my work.                1   2   3   4   5

## **Open-Ended Questions:**

What do you feel is the most positive aspect of working here?

Are there any areas where you think we could improve?

What additional support or resources would help you succeed in your role?

Do you have any suggestions for enhancing our work culture?

Thank you for completing the survey! Your feedback will be used to improve our workplace and support a positive environment for everyone.

# APPENDIX 2

## Sample of a Disciplinary Action Policy

### Policy brief & purpose

Our **Disciplinary Action company policy** explains how we address our employees' misconduct or inadequate performance. Employees must be aware of the consequences of their actions. We use this policy to outline our disciplinary procedure.

### Scope

This policy applies to all our employees.

### Policy elements

The stages that may be followed when discipline is deemed necessary include the following:

1. Verbal warning
2. Corrective Actions/Counseling
3. Official written reprimand
4. Disciplinary meeting with appropriate supervisor or manager
5. Final written warning
6. Detraction of benefits
7. Indefinite suspension or demotion
8. Termination

The nature of the offense must be explained to the employee from the beginning of the procedure. The verbal warning may take the form of a simple oral reprimand but also a full discussion if that is necessary.

The employee must read and sign the written reprimand and final written warning. These documents include the time limit in which an employee must correct their conduct before we take further disciplinary action.

The following scenarios indicate where the disciplinary procedure starts depending on the violation:

**Performance issues.** Disciplinary procedure starts at stage 1. It includes but is not limited to:

- Failure to meet performance objectives.
- Attendance issues.
- Failure to meet deadlines.

**Misdemeanors/One-time minor offense.** Disciplinary procedure starts at stage 1. It includes but is not limited to:

- Rude behavior to customers or partners.
- On-the-job minor mistakes.
- Breach of dress code/open door policy etc.
- Involuntary Discrimination.

**Misconduct/Frequent offender.** Disciplinary procedure starts at stage 5. It includes but is not limited to:

- Lack of response to counseling and corrective actions.

- Lost temper in front of customers or partners.

- On-the-job major mistakes.

- Unwillingness to follow health and safety standards.

**Severe offensive behavior/Felony.** Disciplinary procedure starts at stage 6. It includes but is not limited to:

- Corruption/ Bribery.

- Breach of employment agreement.

- Harassment/ Voluntary discrimination.

- Workplace Violence.

- Embezzlement/Fraud.

- Substance Abuse.

Managers or HR may choose to repeat stages of our disciplinary procedure as appropriate. This decision depends on employees' reaction to our disciplinary procedure, whether they repent their behavior and the nature of their offense.

Our disciplinary procedure begins when there is sufficient evidence to justify it. When there is suspicion or hints of misconduct, managers or HR must investigate the matter first.

Appeals are allowed and must be filed to the next line of management as soon as possible.

HR and managers should document every stage of our disciplinary procedure (except the verbal warning.) If appropriate, include necessary information like evidence, testimonies and employee's progress or improvement.

We are obliged to refrain from disciplinary actions that may constitute retaliatory behavior. A no retaliation company policy will be effective at all times to ensure there is no misuse of our disciplinary procedure.

We have the right to modify this policy or act in any other legal or reasonable way as each case demands. But, we will always enforce discipline in a fair and lawful manner.

**Source:** https://resources.workable.com/disciplinary-action-company-policy

# APPENDIX 3

## Training Needs Assessment Form

### Section 1: Employee Information

Name: _____

Job Title: _____

Department: _____

Supervisor: _____

Date of Assessment: _____

### Section 2: Current Job Competencies

*Please indicate your level of proficiency in the following areas related to your role:*

| Skill/Competency | Proficiency Level | Comments |
|---|---|---|
| Job-specific technical skills | ☐ Beginner<br>☐ Intermediate<br>☐ Advanced | _____ |
| Communication | ☐ Beginner<br>☐ Intermediate<br>☐ Advanced | _____ |
| Problem-solving | ☐ Beginner<br>☐ Intermediate<br>☐ Advanced | _____ |

Time management  ☐ Beginner  _____
                 ☐ Intermediate
                 ☐ Advanced

Customer service ☐ Beginner  _____
                 ☐ Intermediate
                 ☐ Advanced

Team collaboration ☐ Beginner  _____
                   ☐ Intermediate
                   ☐ Advanced

Leadership       ☐ Beginner  _____
                 ☐ Intermediate
                 ☐ Advanced  _____

# Section 3: Training and Development Needs

*Based on your current role, identify any areas where you would benefit from further training:*

1. **Skill Area:** _____

   **Why is this area important to your role?**


2. Skill Area: _____

   **Why is this area important to your role?**


3. Skill Area: _____

   **Why is this area important to your role?**

## Section 4: Career Development Goals

1. **What are your short-term career goals?**

2. **What are your long-term career aspirations?**

3. **Are there any additional skills or certifications that would help you achieve these goals?**

## Section 5: Supervisor/Manager Input

*To be completed by the employee's supervisor or manager:*

1. **What skills would enhance the employee's performance in his/her current role?**

2. **Are there any upcoming changes in the role that will require additional training?**

3. **Recommendations for specific training programs or workshops:**

# Section 6: Additional Comments

**Employee Comments:**

**Supervisor/Manager Comments:**

## Section 7: Signatures

**Employee Signature:** _____

**Date:** _____

**Supervisor/Manager  Signature:** _____
**Date:** _____

# APPENDIX 4

## Sample Results-Oriented Job Description

| | |
|---|---|
| **JOB TITLE:** | **PERSONNEL/HUMAN RESOURCES OFFICER** |
| **DEPARTMENT:** | **HUMAN RESOURCES** |
| **REPORTS TO:** | **HUMAN RESOURCES MANAGER** |
| **JOB(S) SUPERVISED:** | **HR ASSISTANT/CLERK** |
| **JOB PURPOSE:** | **MAINTAINS THE FIRM'S PERSONNEL** |

by

identifying and advertising job vacancies; recruiting candidates; assisting in the selection and assignment of employees.

## ESSENTIAL JOB RESULTS:

1. **MAINTAINS STAFF**

by

identifying current and prospective vacancies; posting notices and advertisements; collecting and screening applications.

2. **PROVIDES INFORMATION**

   by

   advising job applicants on employment requirements; answering questions and requests.

3. **FACILITATES THE RECRUITING PROCESS**

   by

   reviewing candidate inventories.

4. **ARRANGES INTERVIEWS**

   by

   contacting potential applicants.

5. **ENSURES PERSONNEL AVAILABILITY**

   by

   recruiting graduates of universities, colleges, and other educational institutions.

6. **EVALUATES CANDIDATES**

   by

   co-ordinating and participating in selection process.

7. **COMPLETES SELECTION PROCESS**

   by

   notifying applicants of results of competition.

8. **ENSURES COMPLIANCE**

   by

   advising managers and employees on staffing policies and procedures.

9. **MAINTAINS CONFIDENCE AND PROTECTS OPERATIONS**

by

keeping information confidential.

10. **MONITORS RESULTS**

by

supervising and evaluating staff.

11. **MAINTAINS PROFESSIONAL AND TECHNICAL KNOWLEDGE**

by

attending educational workshops; reviewing professional publications; establishing personal networks; participating in professional societies/organizations.

12. **CONTRIBUTES TO TEAM EFFORT**

by

accomplishing related results as needed.

## Job Specifications

- A bachelor's degree or equivalent in a field related to personnel management, such as business administration, industrial relations, commerce or psychology
- Experience in a clerical or administrative position related to personnel administration.

## Career Progression

Progression to Human Resources Manager is possible with additional experience and training.

**Approved by:**_____

**Date:**_____

    **Day  Month  Year**

**Employee's signature**_____

**Date:**_____

    **Day  Month  Year**

# APPENDIX 5

## Sample Exit Interview Form

### ABC Company Exit Interview Form

*(The purpose of this interview is to provide an opportunity for employees to give honest feedback on their experience at ABC. The information gathered will help us to identify areas where we can improve our employee experience. It will take only a few minutes to complete the form).*

Name: _____

Position: _____

Department: _____

Date of Interview: _____

                        Day   Month   Year

## Section 1: Reasons for Leaving

What is your primary reason for leaving ABC Company?

☐ New job opportunity

☐ Career change

☐ Personal reasons

☐ Relocation

☐ Pursuing education

☐ Other (Please specify): _____

Are there any specific aspects of your role or work environment that contributed to your decision?

## Section 2: Job Satisfaction and Experience

How would you rate your overall job satisfaction at ABC Company?

☐ Very Satisfied

☐ Satisfied

☐ Neutral

☐ Dissatisfied

☐ Very Dissatisfied

Please share what you enjoyed most about your role at ABC Company:

Are there areas where you feel the company could improve?

# Section 3: Workplace Relationships and Support

How would you describe your relationship with your manager/supervisor?

☐ Excellent

☐ Good

☐ Fair

☐ Poor

Did you feel supported by the company in achieving your career goals?

☐ Yes

☐ Somewhat

☐ No

Any additional comments on support or workplace relationships?

# Section 4: Recommendations

Do you have any suggestions for how ABC Company can improve employee satisfaction and retention?

Would you consider re-joining ABC Company in the future?

☐ Yes

☐ No

☐ Maybe

**Comments:**

**Thank you for your feedback and contributions to ABC Company. We wish you all the best in your future endeavors!**

# Glossary of HR Terms

**360-Degree Feedback:** A system or process in which employees receive confidential, anonymous feedback from the people who work around them, including peers, managers, and direct reports.

## A

**Absence Management:** The approach and methods an organisation uses to reduce the occurrence and impact of employee absenteeism.

**Accommodation Adjustment:** Changes made to a workplace or the way work is performed to enable an employee with a disability to work effectively.

**Achievement Oriented:** A personal attribute or approach focused on setting and meeting high standards and achieving significant goals.

**Action Plan:** A detailed plan outlining actions needed to reach one or more goals, or to complete a project.

**Agile Working:** A way of working in which an organization empowers its people to work where, when, and how they choose to maximize productivity and deliver the best results.

**Annual Leave:** The amount of time an employee is allowed to be away from work while still receiving pay. This is typically outlined in the employment contract.

**Applicant Tracking System (ATS):** A software application designed to help manage recruitment and hiring processes, including tracking job applicants.

**Appraisal:** A review process where an employee's performance is evaluated, often leading to feedback, development plans, or discussions about career progression.

**Aptitude Test:** A standardized test designed to measure an individual's ability in a particular skill or field of knowledge.

**Arbitration:** A method of resolving disputes outside the courts, where the parties to a dispute refer it to one or more persons and agree to be bound by the arbitration decision.

**Assessment:** The evaluation of the performance, skills, or abilities of an employee or a job applicant.

**Assessment Centre:** A method used in the recruitment process involving a collection of exercises, tests, and interviews to assess the suitability of candidates for a specific role.

**Attrition:** The reduction in staff numbers owing to retirement, resignation, or termination, not replaced by new hires.

# B

Background Check: The process of looking up and compiling criminal records, commercial records, and financial records of an individual or an organization.

**Balanced Scorecard:** A strategic planning and management system used to align business activities to the vision and strategy of the organization, improve internal and external communications, and monitor organizational performance.

**Bandwidth:** Informally used to describe the capacity of an individual or team to take on additional tasks or roles.

**Benchmarking:** The process of comparing one's business processes and performance metrics to industry bests or best practices.

**Bench Strength:** Refers to the capabilities and readiness of potential employees to fill critical roles or leadership positions within the organization.

**Benefits:** Various forms of non-wage compensation provided to employees in addition to their normal wages or salaries, like pensions, health insurance, and holidays.

**Benefits in Kind:** Non-cash benefits provided to employees, such as company cars, private medical insurance, and other non-monetary perks.

**Best Practice:** Techniques or methodologies that, through experience and research, have reliably led to a desired or optimum result.

**Biodata:** Information about an individual's life, work, and career accomplishments; used in recruitment and selection processes.

**Blended Workforce:** A workforce that is made up of employees who are permanent and those who are not, such as contractors, freelancers, or part-time employees.

**Blue-Collar:** Relating to manual work or workers, particularly in industry, as opposed to white-collar office workers.

**Bonus:** A financial reward beyond one's regular salary, often given for achieving certain performance targets or for exceptional work.

**Bonus Scheme:** A plan or system used by businesses to incentivize and reward employees beyond their regular pay.

**Bradford Factor:** A human resources tool used to measure absenteeism.

**Break Clause:** A clause in a contract that allows a person or party to end the contract early.

**Burnout:** A state of physical, emotional, and mental exhaustion caused by prolonged stress and overwork, often resulting in decreased performance and motivation.

**Business Continuity Planning:** The process of creating systems of prevention and recovery to deal with potential threats to an organization.

**Business Ethics:** The study of proper business policies and practices regarding potentially controversial subjects such as corporate governance, insider trading, bribery, discrimination, corporate social responsibility, and fiduciary responsibilities.

**Buy-In:** Agreement or acceptance, often by employees, of a new idea or strategy proposed by management.

# C

**Candidate:** An individual applying for a job or being considered for a specific position.

**Capability Development:** Enhancing the skills and abilities of employees to perform their job roles effectively and to support future business needs.

**Capability Procedure:** A process used by employers to manage employees who are not meeting certain performance standards at work.

**Career Break:** A period when an employee takes an extended leave from his/her career, often for personal reasons such as travel, study, or childcare.

**Career Development:** The lifelong process of managing learning, work, leisure, and transitions in order to move toward a personally determined and evolving preferred future.

**Career Ladder:** The progression of steps, or stages, in an individual's career path within an organization.

**Career Pathing:** The process used by employees to chart a course within an organization for their career path and career development.

**Casual Worker:** Someone who is not contracted to regular hours but works on an 'as needed' basis, often without the same employment rights as full-time staff.

**Change Agent:** An individual or group that helps an organisation transform itself by focusing on such matters as organizational effectiveness, improvement, and development.

**Change Management:** The process, tools, and techniques used to manage the people side of change to achieve a required business outcome.

**Coaching:** A development process where an individual is supported while achieving a specific personal or professional competence or goal.

**Coaching Culture:** A work environment where coaching is a key aspect of how the leaders, managers, and staff engage and develop all employees and themselves.

**Cognitive Ability Test:** A test designed to measure a person's mental capacity or ability to think, reason, and solve problems.

**Collective Agreement:** A written contract negotiated through collective bargaining for employees by one or more trade unions with the management of a company (or with an employers' association), concerning the terms and conditions of employment.

**Collective Bargaining:** The process in which working people, through their unions, negotiate contracts with their employers to determine their terms of employment.

**Commission:** A form of payment to an employee based on the amount of sales that the employee generates.

**Compensatory Rest:** Rest periods which are taken at a later time when an employee has had to skip or reduce his/her regular breaks or rest periods.

**Competency:** A skill or attribute that is required to carry out a job effectively.

**Compromise Agreement:** An agreement, typically arising in the context of an employment dispute, in which the employer and employee reach a mutually agreeable resolution.

**Conflict Resolution:** The process of resolving a dispute or a conflict by meeting at least some of each side's needs and addressing their interests.

**Constructive Dismissal:** A situation where an employee resigns as a result of the employer creating a hostile work environment.

**Contingent Workforce:** A labour pool whose members are hired by an organization on an on-demand basis.

**Contract of Employment:** A legal agreement between an employer and an employee which sets out the employment rights, responsibilities, and duties.

**Core Hours:** The period during the day when employees are expected to be at work, as part of flexible working arrangements.

**Corporate Culture:** The beliefs, behaviours, values, and symbols that a company accepts, generally without thinking about them, and that are passed along by communication and imitation from one generation of employees to another.

**Corporate Governance:** The system of rules, practices, and processes by which a firm is directed and controlled.

**Corporate Social Responsibility (CSR):** A self-regulating business model that helps a company be socially accountable to itself, its stakeholders, and the public.

**Cost of Living Adjustment (COLA):** An increase in income to help employees keep up with inflation.

**Counter Offer:** An offer made in response to a previous offer by the other party during negotiations.

**Creativity and Innovation:** The process of translating an idea or invention into a good or service that creates value or for which customers will pay.

**Critical Success Factors:** The crucial steps companies must take to achieve their goals.

**Cross-Functional Team:** A group of people with different functional expertise working toward a common goal.

**C-Suite:** A term used to collectively refer to a corporation's most important senior executives whose titles start with the letter C, for chief, as in CEO, CFO, COO, etc.

**Culture Fit:** The likelihood that a candidate will reflect and/or be able to adapt to the core beliefs, attitudes, and behaviours that make up an organization.

**CV (Curriculum Vitae):** A detailed written overview of an individual's experience and other qualifications for a job opportunity.

# D

**Data Protection Act:** The law designed to protect personal data stored on computers or in an organized paper filing system.

**Demotion:** The act of reducing an employee's rank or position, often accompanied by a decrease in salary and responsibilities.

**Delegation:** The assignment of responsibility or authority to another person to carry out specific activities, while the person delegating retains ultimate responsibility for the outcome.

**Deliverables:** Tangible or intangible goods or services produced as a result of a project that is intended to be delivered to a customer.

**Development Plan:** A detailed plan outlining an individual's strategy for professional growth, identifying skills to be acquired, knowledge to be gained, and opportunities to be pursued.

**Direct Compensation:** Financial benefits given to employees in the form of salaries, wages, bonuses, and commissions.

**Direct Report:** An employee who is managed directly by another employee, typically by a manager or supervisor.

**Disability:** In the context of HR, it refers to a physical or mental condition that limits a person's movements, senses, or activities, and which may require special accommodations in the workplace.

**Disability Discrimination Act:** Legislation that promotes civil rights for disabled people and protects disabled people from discrimination.

**Disciplinary Procedure:** A formal process for dealing with an employee who is considered to have violated company policies or rules.

**Dismissal:** The act of terminating an employee's contract, often due to misconduct or redundancy.

**Distance Learning:** A way of studying where tuition is carried out over the Internet or by post, without the need to physically attend a school or college.

**Diversity:** The inclusion of individuals from a wide range of backgrounds and identities in the workplace, including race, gender, age, and other characteristics.

**Diversity Management:** The practice of addressing and supporting multiple lifestyles and personal characteristics within a defined group.

**Downsize:** Reducing the number of employees within an organization, often because of economic reasons or organizational restructuring.

**Dress Code:** A set of rules specifying the required manner of dress at the workplace.

**Due Diligence:** The comprehensive appraisal of a business undertaken by a prospective buyer, especially to establish its assets and liabilities and evaluate its commercial potential.

**Duvet Day:** A spontaneous, unscheduled day off given to employees for rest and mental well-being, separate from standard sick or annual leave, emphasizing the importance of mental health in the workplace.

# E

**E-Learning:** Learning conducted via electronic media, typically on the Internet.

**EAP (Employee Assistance Programme):** A work-based intervention program designed to assist employees in resolving personal problems that may be adversely affecting the employee's performance.

**Early Retirement:** The option for an employee to retire before the traditional retirement age, often with reduced pension benefits.

**Employee Advocacy:** The promotion of a company or organization by its staff members.

**Employee Benefits:** Non-wage compensation provided to employees in addition to their normal wages or salaries.

**Earnings Threshold:** The minimum amount employees must earn before they qualify for certain benefits or rights, such as statutory sick pay.

**Employee Engagement:** The emotional commitment the employee has to the organization and its goals, often resulting in improved performance.

**Employee Handbook:** A manual or document that provides information about the company's history, mission, values, policies, procedures, and benefits in a written format.

**Employee Lifecycle:** The different stages an employee goes through during his/her time at an organization, from hiring to retirement or exit.

**Employee Relations:** The management and maintenance of relationships between an employer and its employees.

**Employee Retention:** The ability of an organization to retain its employees.

**Employee Satisfaction:** The level of contentment employees feel about their work, which can affect performance and overall productivity.

**Employee Self-Service:** A system that allows employees to handle many job-related tasks, such as applications for reimbursement, updating personal information, and accessing company information, that would otherwise have to be completed by management or administrative staff.

**Employee Turnover:** The rate at which employees leave a workforce and are replaced.

**Employee Value Proposition (EVP):** A set of associations and offerings provided by an organization in return for the skills, capabilities, and experiences an employee brings to the organization.

**Employer Branding:** The process of promoting a company, or an organization, as the employer of choice to a desired target group.

**Employer of Choice:** A company or organization that is attractive to potential employees because of the quality of the working environment and the benefits it offers.

**Employment Equity:** The employment practices that ensure non-discrimination and promote equality in the workplace.

**Employment Law:** A broad area of law that deals with the rights and duties between employers and workers.

**Empowerment:** Providing employees with the resources, authority, opportunity, and motivation to take initiative and make decisions to solve problems and improve service and performance.

**End of Year Review:** A formal assessment conducted at the end of the year to evaluate an employee's performance, achievements, and areas for development.

**Engagement:** The emotional commitment the employee has to the organization and its goals.

**Equal Opportunities:** The principle of treating all people the same, regardless of their race, sex, sexual orientation, etc., especially in employment.

**Equal Pay:** The concept of labour rights that individuals in the same workplace be given equal pay for work of equal value.

**Equity Theory:** A theory of motivation that focuses on the idea that fairness is a key component in the workplace.

**ERG (Employee Resource Group):** Employee-led groups that focus on shared interests or characteristics, such as gender, ethnicity, religious affiliation, lifestyle, or career interests.

**Ethical Leadership:** The demonstration of normatively appropriate conduct through personal actions and interpersonal relationships, and the promotion of such conduct to followers through two-way communication.

**Exit Interview:** An interview with an employee who is leaving a company, used to gain feedback and understand the reasons for his/her departure.

**Exit Strategy:** A planned approach to exiting a situation, which is usually a business operation, position, or agreement.

**Expatriate:** An employee who is temporarily or permanently residing in a country other than his/her native country, often sent by an employer to work at a foreign branch.

**Experiential Learning:** The process of learning through experience and is more specifically defined as learning through reflection on doing.

# F

**Flexible Benefits:** An employee benefits plan that allows employees to select from a pool of choices, some or all of which may be tax-advantaged.

**Flexible Working:** A working arrangement that allows employees to vary their working hours, location, or pattern of work to suit their personal needs.

**Freelancer:** An individual who works as a self-employed person, rather than for a single employer, often engaged in particular assignments or projects.

**Forced Distribution:** A method of performance appraisal that assigns employees to predefined categories based on their relative performance.

**Full-Time Equivalent (FTE):** A unit that indicates the workload of an employed person in a way that makes workloads or class loads comparable across various contexts.

**Furlough:** A temporary leave of employees owing to special needs of a company, which may be due to economic conditions at a specific employer or in the economy as a whole.

# G

**Garden Leave:** A period during which an employee is paid and remains employed but is instructed to stay away from work, typically used to protect sensitive company information when transitioning out of a role.

**Gender Pay Gap:** The average difference in pay between men and women within a workforce, expressed as a percentage of men's earnings.

**Gig Economy:** A labour market characterized by the prevalence of short-term contracts or freelance work, as opposed to permanent jobs.

**Glass Ceiling:** An unofficially acknowledged barrier to advancement in a profession, especially affecting women and members of minorities.

**Golden Handshake:** A large payment given to a person when he/she leaves a company or retires.

**Golden Parachute:** A substantial benefits package given to top executives if the company is taken over by another firm, and the executives are terminated as a result of the merger or takeover.

**Grade:** The categorization of a particular job based on its level of responsibility and remuneration.

**Grievance Procedure:** A formal process by which an employee can raise a concern, problem, or complaint regarding the workplace.

**Gross Misconduct:** A serious act or behaviour by an employee that justifies immediate dismissal without notice.

# H

**Headcount:** The total number of people employed by an organization at a particular time.

**Head hunter:** A recruiter who seeks out candidates, often for senior positions.

**Health and Safety:** Regulations and procedures intended to prevent accident or injury in workplaces or public environments.

**Hiring Freeze:** A temporary halt in the recruitment process of a company, often due to financial constraints or organizational restructuring.

**Holiday Pay:** Payment for days when employees are not required to work because they are part of their entitled holiday allowance.

**HR (Human Resources):** The division of a business that is charged with finding, screening, recruiting, and training job applicants, as well as administering employee-benefit programs.

**HRIS (Human Resource Information System):** A system used by HR departments to track and manage employee data.

# I

**Inclusion:** The practice or policy of providing equal access to opportunities and resources for people who might otherwise be excluded, such as those having physical or mental disabilities and members of other minority groups.

**Induction:** The process of introducing new employees to a company, including its culture, policies, and the specific duties and responsibilities of their job.

**Industrial Action:** Measures taken by the workforce or trade union to put pressure on management, typically involving a strike or work-to-rule.

**In-Service Training:** Training that is provided by an employer during the course of employment to improve the skills and knowledge of employees.

**Interim:** An employee or role that is intended to cover a position temporarily.

**Intern:** A student or trainee who works, sometimes without pay, in order to gain work experience or satisfy requirements for a qualification.

# J

**Job Description:** A formal account of an employee's responsibilities and the specific duties that employee is expected to perform in his/her role.

**Job Evaluation:** The process of analyzing and assessing various jobs systematically to ascertain their relative worth in an organization.

**Job Share:** An employment arrangement where typically two people are retained on a part-time or reduced-time basis to perform a job normally fulfilled by one person working full-time.

# K

**Key Performance Indicator (KPI):** A set of quantifiable measures that a company uses to gauge or compare performance in terms of meeting its strategic and operational goals.

**Knowledge Transfer:** The process by which experienced employees share or distribute their knowledge, skills, and behaviours to the employees replacing them.

# L

**Layoff:** A temporary suspension or permanent termination of employment of an employee or, more commonly, a group of employees for business reasons, such as personnel management or downsizing an organization.

**Learning and Development:** A function within HR that focuses on the improvement of skills and knowledge in employees through various forms of training and education.

**Leave of Absence:** A period of time that one must be away from one's primary job while maintaining the status of employee.

**Living Wage:** A wage that is high enough to maintain a normal standard of living.

**Long Service Award:** An award given to employees in recognition of a significant period of service to the company.

## M

**Maternity Leave:** A period of absence from work granted to a mother before and after the birth of her child.

**Mentor:** An experienced and trusted adviser who provides guidance and support to a less experienced colleague, often in a professional setting.

**Merit Increase:** An increase in salary given to an employee based on his/her performance.

**Minimum Wage:** The lowest remuneration that employers can legally pay their workers.

**Misconduct:** Improper or unacceptable behaviour or wrongdoing, especially by an employee or professional person.

**Mobile Working:** Working away from a fixed office location and being able to work on the go.

## N

**National Insurance:** Mandatory payments made by employees and employers in some countries, used to fund various benefits.

**Net Pay:** The amount of an employee's wages after deductions, such as taxes and retirement contributions, have been subtracted.

**Notice Period:** The length of time that an employee must work after resigning or being dismissed.

# O

**Occupational Health:** The field of healthcare that is concerned with the health of employees in the workplace.

**Offboarding:** The process of transitioning employees out of a company when they leave.

**Onboarding:** The process of integrating a new employee into the organization and its culture.

**Overtime:** Time worked beyond the standard hours set by the company's policy.

# P

**Part-Time:** Working less than the full-time hours, typically by working fewer days per week.

**Paternity Leave:** A period of time that a father is allowed to be away from his work after the birth of his child.

**Pay Grade:** A step within a compensation system that defines the amount of pay an employee will receive.

**Payroll:** The total amount of wages paid by a company to its employees and other workers.

**PDP (Personal Development Plan):** A document created by an individual to detail his/her development goals and the actions needed to achieve them, often in a professional context.

**Performance Improvement Plan:** A tool used by employers to give struggling employees the opportunity to succeed while still holding them accountable for past performance.

**Performance Management:** The process by which managers and employees work together to plan, monitor, and review an employee's work objectives and overall contribution to the organization.

**Perk:** An extra benefit or bonus, often non-monetary, that is given to employees in addition to their regular salary or wages.

**Personal Leave:** Time taken off from work for personal reasons, which can include family needs, personal emergencies, or other personal matters.

**Phased Retirement:** A retirement plan that allows employees to reduce their working hours over a period of time before completely retiring.

**Payment in Lieu of Notice (PILON):** A financial compensation paid by an employer to employees instead of having them work their notice period upon termination of employment.

**Pipelining:** The process of creating a pool of candidates who are qualified for future job openings.

**Placement:** The assignment of a person to a job or position.

**Position:** A particular post within an organization, typically with specific duties and responsibilities.

**Pre-employment Screening:** The process of verifying the qualifications of job applicants before they are hired.

**Probation:** A trial period during which an employee's suitability for a job is evaluated by the employer.

**Pro Rata:** A method of calculating salaries and benefits based on the proportion of hours worked, ensuring part-time or temporary employees receive fair compensation relative to full-time equivalents

**Psychometric Testing:** A standard and scientific method used to measure individuals' mental capabilities and behavioural style, often used in the recruitment process.

**Public Holiday:** A holiday generally established by law and is usually a non-working day during the year.

# Q

**Quiet Quitting:** The act of an employee disengaging from his/her work and doing the minimum required without formally resigning.

# R

**Redeployment:** The process of moving an employee to a different role or department within the organization.

**Redundancy:** The situation in which an employer reduces its workforce because a job or jobs are no longer needed.

**Referral Programme:** A system where current employees are rewarded for referring suitable candidates for job openings within the organization.

**Remote Working:** Working from a location other than the employer's workplace, often from home or a location of the employee's choice.

**Resignation:** The act of giving notice of your intention to leave your job and terminate your employment contract.

**Restructuring:** The act of reorganizing the legal, ownership, operational, or other structures of a company for the purpose of making it more profitable or better organized for its present needs.

**Retention:** The ability of a company to retain its employees and reduce turnover.

**Retirement:** The action or fact of leaving one's job and ceasing to work, typically upon reaching a certain age.

**Return to Work:** The process of reintegration or returning to work after an absence, such as after maternity leave, sickness, or a career break.

**Right to Work:** The legal confirmation that a person is entitled to work in a particular country.

**Role:** The function assumed or part played by a person in a particular situation, especially in a job.

# S

**Sabbatical:** A period of leave granted to an employee for study or travel, traditionally every seventh year, for a duration that can vary, often not paid.

**Safe Working Conditions:** Workplace environments that do not pose a risk of serious harm to employees.

**Salary Band:** A range of pay levels for employees holding similar job titles or positions, reflecting different levels of skills or experience.

**Salary Sacrifice:** An arrangement where employees give up part of their salary in return for some form of non-cash benefit.

**Secondment:** The temporary transfer of an employee to another job or post within the same or another organization.

**Self-Employed:** People who work for themselves rather than for an employer.

**Severance Pay:** Money paid to employees when they leave a company, often based on the length of employment.

**Shift Work:** A work schedule that is not the traditional 9-to-5, often involving evening or overnight hours.

**Short-Term Contract:** An employment contract that lasts for a limited period of time.

**Sickness Absence:** Time off taken by an employee because of illness.

**Skills Gap:** The difference between the skills required for a job and the skills possessed by the applicant or employee.

**SMART Goals:** Specific, Measurable, Achievable, Relevant, and Time-bound objectives set to guide performance and development.

**Social Recruiting:** The use of social media networks and websites to find, attract, and hire talent.

**Staff:** The group of people who work for an organization.

**Stakeholder:** Any person, group, or organization that has an interest in the performance and activities of a company.

**Statutory Sick Pay:** The minimum amount an employer is legally required to pay an employee, such as statutory sick pay or maternity pay.

**Stay Interview:** A meeting with employees to discuss their reasons for staying with the organization and any potential issues that might cause them to leave.

**STEM (Science, Technology, Engineering, and Mathematics):** An educational and occupational classification covering areas of study and work in science, technology, engineering, and mathematics fields.

**Stipend:** A fixed, regular sum paid as a salary or allowance, often to an intern or apprentice.

**Succession Planning:** The process of identifying and developing new leaders who can replace old leaders when they leave, retire, or die.

# T

**Talent Acquisition:** The process of finding and acquiring skilled human labour for organizational needs and to meet any labour requirement.

**Talent Management:** The ongoing process of developing and retaining an organization's workforce.

**Talent Pool:** A database of candidates who are qualified to assume specific roles within a company when they become available.

**Tax Code:** A tax code is a series of numbers and letters used by employers or pension providers to determine the amount of Income Tax to deduct from an individual's earnings or pension.

**Team Building:** Activities and exercises designed to improve interpersonal relations and teamwork within a group.

**Temporary Work:** Employment that is expected to last for a limited period of time, often used to cover short-term needs of the employing organization.

**Termination:** The act of ending the employment of an employee or a group of employees.

**Time off in Lieu (TOIL):** Time off in compensation for extra hours worked, also known as 'comp time'.

**Time Management:** The ability to use one's time effectively or productively, especially at work.

**Timesheet:** A record used to track the number of hours worked by an employee.

**Turnover:** The rate at which employees leave a workforce and are replaced, often expressed as a percentage of the total workforce.

# U

**Underemployment:** A situation where individuals are working in a job that is insufficient in some important way for them, such as not utilizing their skills, or working fewer hours than they would prefer.

**Unfair Dismissal:** The firing of an employee without just cause.

**Union:** An organized association of workers formed to protect and further their rights and interests.

**Upskilling:** The process of learning new or improving existing skills, often for career development purposes.

# V

**Variable Pay:** Compensation that is not fixed and may vary according to performance or results achieved.

**Voluntary Redundancy:** A situation where employees agree to leave their jobs in exchange for financial compensation, often as part of a cost-cutting strategy.

# W

**Wage:** The fixed regular payment, typically paid on a daily or weekly basis, made by an employer to an employee, especially a manual or unskilled worker.

**Wellbeing:** The state of b eing comfortable, healthy, or happy in the workplace.

**Whistle-blower:** An employee who exposes any kind of information or activity within an organization that is deemed illegal, unethical, or not correct.

**White-Collar:** Pertaining to the work done or those who work in an office or other professional environment.

**Without Prejudice Conversation:** A legally protected discussion between parties in a dispute, where statements made cannot be used as evidence in court, allowing for candid negotiation and resolution attempts

**Work-Life Balance:** The equilibrium between an individual's work life and personal life.

**Work Permit:** An official document giving a foreigner permission to take a job in a country.

**Work Shadowing:** A work experience where a person learns about a job by walking through the work day as a shadow to a competent worker.

**Workforce Planning:** The process of analyzing the current workforce, determining future workforce needs, and identifying the gap between the present and the future in order to implement solutions.

**Working Conditions:** The environment in which an individual or staff works, including but not limited to things like safety, amenities, physical demands, and legal rights.

**Working Time Regulations:** Regulations that govern how long employees can work, including limits on the average working week, statutory entitlement to paid leave, and the regulation of night work.

**Workplace Bullying:** Repeated, unreasonable actions of individuals or a group directed towards an employee or a group of employees which create a risk to health and safety.

**Workplace Discrimination:** Unfair or unequal treatment of an employee or group of employees based on personal characteristics such as age, gender, race, religion, or disability.

**Workplace Harassment:** Unwanted conduct affecting the dignity of men and women in the workplace, which may be related to age, sex, race, disability, religion, nationality, or any personal characteristic of the individual.

www.ingramcontent.com/pod-product-compliance
Lightning Source LLC
Chambersburg PA
CBHW040754220326
41597CB00029BA/4777

9 781069 008664